T0269814

BAPHOMET
REVEALED

ALSO BY HEATHER LYNN

Evil Archeology

The Anunnaki Connection

BAPHOMET REVEALED

Mysteries and Magic of the Sacred Icon

HEATHER LYNN, PHD

This edition first published in 2024 by New Page Books,
an imprint of Red Wheel/Weiser, LLC

With offices at:
65 Parker Street, Suite 7
Newburyport, MA 01950
www.redwheelweiser.com

ISBN: 978-1-63748-019-9

Library of Congress Cataloging-in-Publication Data available upon request.

Cover design by Sky Peck Design
Cover illustration by iStock
Interior by Maureen Forys, Happenstance Type-O-Rama
Typeset in Change, Adelon, and IM Fell Double Pica Pro

Printed in the United States of America
IBI

10 9 8 7 6 5 4 3 2 1

To the seekers of shadows and the workers of Light,
From the realm of chaos, where opposites unite,
Your Path is inscribed in the cosmos above,
In this aeon of conflict, may you always choose Love.

CONTENTS

ACKNOWLEDGMENTS

I want to extend my heartfelt gratitude to the excellent Michael Pye at Red Wheel/Weiser for his unwavering support. Michael's dedication, guidance, and belief in the importance of this work have been invaluable, and I am truly fortunate to have had him as my editor. To the entire team at Red Wheel/Weiser, thank you for your professionalism, expertise, and passion for preserving and disseminating arcane wisdom. Your collective efforts have made it possible for me to share this exploration and other essential works with a broader audience.

INTRODUCTION
The Mystery of Baphomet

*All miracles are promised to faith, and what is faith
except the audacity of will which does not hesitate in the
darkness, but advances towards the light in spite of all
ordeals, and surmounting all obstacles?*

—ÉLIPHAS LÉVI

Of all arcane symbols, few provoke as much fascination and controversy as the complex and multilayered symbol Baphomet. The origin and history of this most infamous of "devilish" images may surprise you. The icon of Baphomet, so often linked with profane devil worship, originated from the mind of a French Catholic priest—a deeply faithful man known as Éliphas Lévi. Far from being a symbol of malevolence, the figure Lévi drew was intended to represent love, unity, and spiritual wisdom. Lévi termed this blend of mysticism and esoteric understanding of the faith *true Catholicism*, keeping in mind that *catholic* comes from the Greek word *katholikos*, which means "universal" or "according to the whole." Early Christian writers, such as Ignatius of Antioch, used this term to describe the Christian Church as universal, united, and spread throughout the world, in contrast to individual local congregations. In this context, the term was not exclusively associated with what later became the Roman Catholic Church. However, in a secular or nonreligious context, the lowercase word *catholic* can refer to a broadness of view or taste, a wide-ranging inclusivity, or a general comprehensiveness. Thus, the symbol of Baphomet embodies a holistic principle, a transformative "third element," an alchemical or Hegelian synthesis that goes beyond mere dualities.

For someone raised in the Roman Catholic tradition and who has converted and been baptized into Anglo-Catholicism, I find the multilayered symbolism of Baphomet both deeply unsettling and strangely comforting. My initial exposure to the symbol, like that of many others, was veiled in misunderstanding and caution, a response sculpted by a lifetime of theological conditioning. However, upon entering the fields of cognitive archaeology and comparative religious studies, I felt a strong resonance with Éliphas Lévi's quest for a more primordial understanding of spirituality—what he might refer to as the "true religion" (Lévi 1861). Lévi's works resonate with me as I grapple with the dissonances and harmonies between the teachings of my upbringing and the deeper, more universal insights offered by the perennial philosophy, magic, and alchemy. Like Lévi, I view these often misunderstood and maligned areas of study not as contradictory to faith but as different expressions of the same cosmic language—each serving as a syllabus in the grand curriculum of universal wisdom. What Manly P. Hall (1928) termed "the secret teachings of all ages" aligns impeccably with this view. Each age, each culture, each religion comes into contact with fragments of this perennial wisdom and tries to interpret it within the limitations of its historical and cultural vocabulary.

There was a time when the image of Baphomet, with its disconcerting blend of the animal, human, and divine, would send chills down my spine. However, as Joseph Campbell once so eloquently stated, "The cave you fear to enter holds the treasure you seek." My journey into these caves of antiquity, into the dark recesses of myth and archaic symbolism, has been a transformative process. While writing my book *Evil Archaeology*, I learned from the lessons of antiquity as well as modern-day exorcists that fear is the opposite of faith. The biblical Psalm 23:4 comes to mind: "Yea, though I walk through the valley of the shadow of death, I will fear no evil: for thou art with me; thy rod and thy staff they comfort me" (KJV).

So why do we fear? And why do such symbols as Baphomet unsettle us? Perhaps it is because fear is the chain that binds us to ignorance; it is what prevents us from liberating our perceptions and thus, our spirit. I have come to realize that fear is a mechanism of control, whether by religious institutions or broader societal norms. But once you cast away the fear and walk confidently into the proverbial valley, the illumination of understanding lights your way. I do not fear images, symbols, or the complex pages of arcane books because they are, to me, mirrors reflecting aspects of a greater truth. Thus, I extend an invitation to you: be not afraid. Engage in this exploration with an open heart and a fearless mind, for faith is the lamp that dispels darkness and guides us toward the truth.

Lévi, whom we will examine more closely in this book, enriched his iconic illustration of Baphomet with this ageless wisdom. In presenting us with such a challenging and multi-layered symbol, he encourages us to confront and question our deepest fears and apprehensions. He extends an invitation to peer into the complexities of the symbol, to go beyond the initial revulsion or fear, and discover the harmonizing elements that reside within. Lévi's Baphomet portrays not just dualities—masculine and feminine, terrestrial and celestial—but also subtle "thirds," such as the torch of enlightenment wedged between Baphomet's horns, which transcend and integrate these polarities into a harmonious whole. Moreover, Lévi elucidated the intricate relationship between the exoteric and the esoteric aspects of magickal symbols and texts. While the exoteric provides an accessible but superficial understanding, the esoteric harbors a hidden depth unlocked only through initiatory experience. Much like a gateway from the exoteric to the esoteric, Baphomet serves as an emblem embodying multiple layers of meaning: both the outward appearances that provoke the public imagination and the arcane wisdom available to those willing to engage in the deeper study of self-exploration.

As we peek under the veil of Baphomet's rich historical narrative, the symbol becomes a mirror, reflecting the duality inherent within us, resonating with the unseen "other" that resides in our subconscious. Guided by these multifaceted lenses, this book endeavors to lead you through an exploratory journey, for at the crux of our identity lies a profound duality, a concept so aptly captured by Carl Jung, the Swiss psychiatrist and founder of analytical psychology. His understanding of the human psyche hinges on the notion that in each of us, there is an "other," an unconscious aspect of ourselves that perceives reality in a manner distinct from our conscious self. This "other," often elusive and misunderstood, becomes the focal point of our exploration into the mysterious symbol. The icon, in its intricate design, encompasses a realm of paradoxes, symbolizing both unity and opposition, the amalgamation of the spiritual and the material, the human and the divine, and the eternal dance between knowledge and mystery. It is no wonder that the figure of Baphomet arouses a sense of apprehension in many; its use in modern times has been appropriated to symbolize unsettling themes of satanic worship and diabolical practices. The dread it engenders today is partly a product of its contemporary associations, which stray far from its original esoteric intent.

It is time to allay these fears by making the unknown known. In this book, we strip away the power fear holds over us, replacing it with understanding. The exploration henceforth is not just about unearthing the layers of meanings assigned to Baphomet over the centuries, but also about introspection and understanding our own complexities mirrored in their symbolism. Thus, in our analysis of Baphomet, we might also find ourselves coming closer to understanding the "other" within us, embracing the plurality of our own identity. We embark on this quest with a spirit of open inquiry and scholarly rigor, acknowledging our subject's inherent complexity and elusive nature. As we will find, Baphomet is not easily pinned down to a single interpretation or origin story. Instead, Baphomet exists as a symbol depicting both our deepest fears and our highest aspirations.

Where, then, does this arcane symbol come from, and what does it truly represent? These are some of the questions that will guide our investigation. Our quest will take us back to the Knights Templar, who are often credited with the creation of Baphomet, and further back still, seeking out potential connections to ancient esoteric traditions. In pursuit of understanding, we will scrutinize the historical record, considering both facts and fiction, as the truth may lie somewhere in between. Our

journey will then lead us into the realm of Gnosticism and Freemasonry, exploring the symbiotic relationship between these
esoteric traditions and Baphomet. What role did these currents
of thought play in the evolution of Baphomet? To what extent
have they shaped the interpretations and practices surrounding
this mysterious and sometimes controversial figure?

A significant component of our investigation requires an
in-depth examination of the aforementioned Éliphas Lévi. Born
Alphonse Louis Constant, Lévi was a prominent French occultist and pivotal figure in the nineteenth-century occult revival
whose influence on our current understanding of Baphomet
can hardly be overstated. It was Lévi, after all, who presented us
with the most iconic and widely recognized image of Baphomet
from his seminal work, *Dogme et Rituel de la Haute Magie* (Dogma
and the Ritual of Transcendental Magic), first published in two
volumes between 1854 and 1856, then translated into English in
1896 by Arthur Edward Waite as *Transcendental Magic, Its Doctrine and Ritual*. Lévi's interpretation drew upon a broad range
of philosophical, religious, and occult influences, resulting in a
richly layered symbol that offers multiple avenues for analysis
and interpretation. His descriptions have arguably served as the
primary compass guiding our collective understandings of this
iconic symbol. It is an image that combines elements of Eastern
and Western mysticism, pagan and Christian symbolism, and
metaphysical concepts from an array of esoteric traditions.

Sometimes referred to as the "Sabbatic Goat" or the "Goat
of Mendes," Lévi's Baphomet is an intricate study in symbolic
layering: a composite figure; an androgynous goat-headed being
that embodies both masculine and feminine attributes, reflecting the concept of the divine hermaphrodite; a synthesis of

binary opposites (Lévi 1855/1896). The figure's arms are inscribed with the Latin words *Solve* and *Coagula*, signifying the alchemical process of dissolution and coagulation, or in broader terms, the transformative process of destruction and creation (ibid.). The upward-pointing pentagram on Baphomet's forehead, often associated with spirit ruling over the four elements, suggests spiritual dominion. At the same time, the torch between the horns symbolizes enlightenment and the illumination of the intellect (ibid.). To Lévi, Baphomet was not a god or an idol, but a symbol encapsulating the equilibrium of the opposites and an embodiment of the "astral light"—a metaphysical force that, according to him, pervades the universe and serves as a medium for magical operations (ibid.). Lévi wrote: "Baphomet is not a God; He is the sign of initiation. . . . It is the Initiate's responsibility to transform the nightmare into a vision; the Baphomet must be made to serve, or the applicant will be possessed by him" (ibid., 111). This now-famous portrayal offers a way to appreciate Baphomet as a symbolic bridge between dualities—male and female, good and evil, human and animal, physical and spiritual—and a personification of equilibrium and unity in a world often defined by division and dichotomy. Within Lévi's detailed writings, we find a Baphomet imbued with various interpretive possibilities, opening many avenues for further exploration.

To better understand Baphomet, this book will dig deeper into the life, philosophy, and works of Lévi himself, as he was not merely an observer, but a keen participant in the esoteric traditions of his time. His ideas about magic, symbolism, and the nature of reality were all woven into his depiction of Baphomet. As we examine the depth of Lévi's influence, we also gain insight into the broader cultural and philosophical currents of nineteenth-century Europe. Understanding the context in which he constructed his image of Baphomet helps us see this symbol not only as a personal creation but also as a product of its time—a reflection of the era's struggles, aspirations, and understandings. Lévi's Baphomet became an archetype of dualities reconciled and an emblem of esoteric wisdom. It served as a powerful representation of the perceived unity underlying apparent opposites, a key concept in Hermetic thought: as above, so below. By reconciling seeming contradictions within a single symbol, Lévi's Baphomet epitomizes the possibility of harmony within multiplicity, of unity within diversity. This concept remains central to many esoteric and occult philosophies to this day. However, it is crucial to note that Lévi's Baphomet is just one interpretation of the symbol. Lévi's specific cultural and historical context, along with his personal biases and interpretations, shaped his understanding of Baphomet. Thus, while Lévi's Baphomet provides a robust and influential interpretation of the symbol, it is far from the only possible interpretation.

Venturing further into its origins and meanings, we encounter a path intersected by the Knights Templar—a clandestine order steeped in secrecy and surrounded by whispered tales of heresy and hidden knowledge. Theories on Baphomet's significance to the Templars vary, with some characterizing it as a revered idol and others portraying it as a symbol of esoteric knowledge and divine enlightenment. These divergent views underscore the allure and complexity that enshroud Baphomet, beckoning us to venture into ancient texts and examine historical accounts to understand the myth and life of Baphomet. What secrets did the Templars safeguard? Did they possess esoteric wisdom that intertwined with the symbol of Baphomet? More importantly, what drew them to this enigmatic figure? Was it a mere representation of their beliefs, or did it hold a profound power that fueled their ascent to power or perhaps their demise? To answer these questions and more, we must embark on a journey that transcends time and unveils a world brimming with intrigue, entangling us in a web of mysteries waiting to be deciphered.

The Knights Templar, established in the mid-twelfth century, were primarily viewed as one of the most potent Catholic military orders of their time (Barber 2012). Initially recognized for their martial prowess and economic acumen, the Templars rapidly expanded their influence beyond their Christian kingdoms, leading some scholars to suggest that they were the first multinational corporation (Ralls 2003). However, the Templars' downfall began when King Philip IV of France exploited their decline to expunge his debts, leading Pope Clement V, under mounting pressure, to dissolve the order (Nicholson 2011). As the Templars' influence waned, troubling rumors surfaced, hinting at a darker aspect to the order. One of the most pervasive rumors involved the Templars' supposed worship of Baphomet instead of the Christian God (Partner 1990). After being interrogated and severely tortured, the Templars eventually confessed, yet their depictions of Baphomet varied considerably (Barber 1993). In his book *The Knights Templar and Their Myth*, Peter Partner (1990) suggests that this confession was likely coerced under extreme duress. Despite the numerous accounts, no concrete evidence from the period conclusively links the Templars to Baphomet worship (Frale 2011). Nevertheless, we will examine the original court transcripts in the upcoming chapter.

Another hypothesis suggests the Knights Templar, stationed in Crusader states, incorporated Islamic doctrine into their belief system, effectively committing heresy in the eyes of their medieval Christian contemporaries. The name *Baphomet* itself might have originated from the Old French term for Muhammad, *Mahomet*, indicating a transformation of the Islamic prophet's name into a false deity. The Templars' association with Baphomet could also be explained by Gnostic beliefs, implying polytheistic practices within the order (Partner 1990). Joseph von Hammer-Purgstall, an Austrian Orientalist, further perpetuated the theory of Baphomet as an androgynous deity. According to Hammer-Purgstall (1818/2017), Baphomet represents a profound connection to ancient mystical traditions and esoteric knowledge. He theorized that Baphomet is rooted in the ancient deity Abraxas, a figure associated with both Gnostic and Hermetic philosophies. Embracing this theory opens up a fascinating realm of exploration, where Baphomet becomes a symbol of transcendence and enlightenment, an interpretation very different from that of today's casual viewer. The notion of Baphomet as a conduit to divine wisdom and esoteric teachings aligns with the belief that hidden knowledge exists, waiting to be discovered by those who seek its truth. Moreover, by connecting Baphomet to Abraxas, Hammer-Purgstall emphasized the concept of unity in duality (ibid.). But who is Abraxas and why would he have been associated with Baphomet?

Abraxas is a mystical figure that holds a significant place in various ancient belief systems and philosophical traditions, including the aforementioned Gnosticism and Hermeticism, as well as other esoteric teachings. The name *Abraxas* is believed to have originated from the Greek word *abrazo*, meaning "I create" or "I am the beginning." The worship of Abraxas can be traced back to the Hellenistic period. He gained popularity during the early Christian era, particularly among certain Gnostic sects. In Gnostic traditions, Abraxas is considered a divine being that exists beyond the confines of the physical realm, embodying the fusion of heavenly and earthly elements. He is often depicted as a composite creature, combining the body of a human with the head of a rooster and serpentine legs. This hybrid form symbolizes the integration of diverse and opposing forces within the universe. Abraxas represents the unity of dualities, encompassing both light and darkness, creation and destruction, good and evil. As a result, Abraxas transcends conventional moral dichotomies, emphasizing the concept of totality and the reconciliation of opposites. This notion aligns with the idea that true enlightenment and spiritual awakening come from embracing and harmonizing the diverse aspects of existence.

In addition to his association with Gnosticism, Abraxas found resonance within the Hermetic tradition. Hermeticism, a philosophical and mystical system attributed to Hermes Trismegistus, emphasizes the pursuit of spiritual enlightenment through the understanding of universal principles and the unity of all things. Abraxas, with his encompassing nature and synthesis of opposing forces, is a symbol of mystical unity, transcending dualities and inviting individuals to seek a deeper understanding of the universe and themselves. He represents the profound wisdom that arises from reconciling seemingly conflicting forces, embracing the totality of existence, and recognizing the divine interplay of light and darkness, creation and destruction.

Hammer-Purgstall's theory, by linking Baphomet to the ancient deity Abraxas and the realms of hidden wisdom, presents a compelling perspective. In this view, Baphomet represents the unity and harmony found within the coexistence of seemingly opposing forces, encouraging us to embrace the totality of existence. Hammer-Purgstall sees Baphomet as a symbol that transcends religious and cultural boundaries. It becomes a universal emblem of esoteric knowledge and spiritual transformation, inviting individuals from various traditions to find common ground in their pursuit of higher truths. While Hammer-Purgstall's approach is largely speculative and thereby subject to interpretation, by understanding this theory, we open ourselves to a profound exploration of mystical traditions and esoteric teachings, unlocking the potential for personal growth, enlightenment, and a deeper appreciation for the symbol that is Baphomet.

According to Hammer-Purgstall's interpretation, Baphomet represents the harmonious integration of both masculine and feminine energies and offers a profound symbolism of balance and unity, transcending the conventional boundaries of gender and embracing the inherent duality within all of us. Baphomet's androgynous nature invites us to explore the depths of our own beings, transcending societal norms and expectations. It challenges us to embrace our inner masculine and feminine qualities, acknowledging that true self-realization emerges from the integration of these seemingly contrasting aspects. In doing so, we open ourselves to a richer understanding of the divine mysteries that Baphomet represents.

Hammer-Purgstall's view offers an intriguing perspective, but, as noted, it must be approached with caution due to its highly speculative nature. Much of his theory is based on subjective interpretations and extrapolations from limited historical evidence. The study of ancient religions and esoteric traditions is a complex and challenging field, often requiring careful analysis and scholarly scrutiny. The meaning of Baphomet has been a topic of debate and speculation among scholars, occultists, and researchers for many years, fueled by the lack of concrete historical evidence and the elusive nature of Baphomet's origins. While Hammer-Purgstall's ideas can serve as a starting point for exploration and contemplation, this study will consider alternative viewpoints and cross-reference other reliable sources to assemble a more complete view of Baphomet and what this symbol can teach us about the times in which we are currently living.

As we consider the true meaning and purpose of Baphomet, it is essential to appreciate the depth and breadth of the symbol, to recognize the vast array of possible interpretations, and to understand that our perception of Baphomet, as with all symbols, is inevitably shaped by our own biases, experiences, and contexts. This broader exploration allows us to view Baphomet as a living symbol—one that is continually evolving, as each generation and each individual engages with it in new ways, bringing their own perspectives, questions, and insights to the ongoing dialogue. Through this process, we seek not only to better understand Baphomet but to deepen our understanding of ourselves, our culture, and the esoteric traditions that continue to shape our worldview. Thus, as we delve into the depths of Baphomet's symbolism, our journey will be as much an inward exploration as an outward one—a journey into the heart of human understanding and the liminal spaces where myth, symbol, and psyche intersect.

This book is not an apologist's defense of Baphomet, nor is it an indictment. It is, instead, an honest examination of the origin, history, and meaning of this provocative symbol. As with most things occult, there are hidden truths and surprising secrets that were meant to be known by a select few. This elitist worldview keeps ancient wisdom shrouded in mystery and deprives us of an understanding not only of the past but of the world in which we currently live. Our contemporary world was built upon the crumbled ruins of human narratives, from which misunderstandings, both honest and dishonest, inevitably arise. As we sift through the buried meanings, we will uncover the truth about the Baphomet symbol. Throughout this textual excavation of ancient symbols, we will turn our gaze to the ways in which Baphomet has been appropriated and redefined by modern Satanism and countercultural movements. This part of Baphomet's journey raises compelling questions about the nature of religious symbolism and the power dynamics of cultural appropriation and will reflect on the implications of Baphomet's dual nature. Can this strange-looking figure challenge our notions of good and evil, offering a more nuanced view of these concepts? Can Baphomet, as a symbol, provide a new lens through which to view the human condition—a lens that recognizes the inherent complexity and paradox of our nature?

These are questions that cut to the heart of why Baphomet continues to captivate our collective imagination. They are questions that invite us, as seekers of understanding, to look beyond the surface and challenge our assumptions. We stand at the threshold of a profound journey—one that beckons us to explore the myth, magick, and life of Baphomet. With each page turned, we will unlock hidden doors of wisdom and lift the veil of the arcane. While this book may challenge your faith, I hope that, once you've finished reading, your faith will be strengthened or, at the very least, you will gain a new understanding of a powerful symbol—one anchored in alchemical wisdom and illumination. As German philosopher Friedrich Nietzsche boldly stated, "There are two different types of people in the world: those who want to know, and those who want to believe." You may *believe* that Baphomet is just an image of the devil, but after reading this book, you will *know* the truth: Baphomet is not a mere shadow of darkness, but rather a symbol of the true light of Illumination.

Chapter 1

FROM MISPRONUNCIATION TO MYSTERY
The Templar Origins of Baphomet

Heresies are experiments in
man's unsatisfied search for truth.

—H. G. WELLS,
English novelist, journalist, and futurist

The Knights Templar, a medieval Catholic military order founded in 1118 CE, holds a prominent place in the annals of history that continues to engage the curiosity of scholars, enthusiasts, and those intrigued by the mysteries of the past. Emerging during the fervor of the Crusades, this order of warrior monks quickly grew in influence and power, creating an lasting mark on the religious, political, and economic landscapes of the era. Their history is intertwined with countless theories, speculations, and rumors that have given rise to a mythos as enduring as the fortified castles they once constructed. At the core of our exploration will be an examination of the potential origins of Baphomet, an entity that, according to certain theories, was allegedly venerated by the Templars. The name *Baphomet* surfaced during the trials of the Templars and has since been a focal point of conjecture and scholarly debate. Although historical evidence remains elusive, this figure has been variously interpreted as a symbol of esoteric wisdom, a cipher for ancient knowledge, and a scapegoat fabricated by the order's enemies.

Tracing the Templars' journey, we will investigate the order's origins, studying the circumstances under which they arose during a time of intense religious conflict. We will observe their notable achievements and consider how, within a relatively short amount of time, they managed to accrue immense wealth and influence. The Templars were architects of some of the period's most significant financial systems, effectively pioneering techniques that would lay the foundation for modern banking. Yet the order's dramatic fall from grace, leading to their dissolution in 1312 CE, is equally noteworthy. We will look at the factors leading to their downfall, focusing on the dramatic trials that ensued after their arrest in 1307 CE, which led to sensational accusations of heresy, blasphemy, and the alleged worship of Baphomet.

Even though the Knights Templar as an order ceased to exist over seven centuries ago, their enduring legacy continues to spark our collective fascination. In media and popular culture, the Templars are often depicted as guardians of holy relics or bearers of arcane knowledge. The idea of the Templars as spiritual soldiers engaged in a secret, mystical war has proven to be an irresistible narrative that has fueled countless works of fiction and conspiracy theories alike. In essence, our journey will provide an in-depth exploration of the Templars not merely as a historical military order, but as an eternal symbol of the mysterious, the hidden, and the perennially unknown. As we unravel their complex legacy, we may find that the figure of Baphomet serves as a mirror, reflecting our own fascination with the hidden aspects of history and the enduring appeal of the esoteric.

Dawn of the Templars

Just two decades following the First Crusade's conclusion that saw the defeat of Muslim forces and the capture of Antioch and Jerusalem (Newman 2007), a small group of French knights, led by Hugues de Payens and Godfrey de Saint-Omer, established the order known as the Knights Templar. Their noble purpose revolved around ensuring the safety of pilgrims bound for the Holy Sepulchre (Barber 1993). King Baldwin II, the recently enthroned ruler of Jerusalem, provided these knights with accommodations adjacent to the sacred site of Solomon's Temple, inspiring their name (Newman 2007). The order was legitimized in 1128, with formal approval from the Council of Troyes and the pope himself. Saint Bernard, a figure of reverence, established a rule that committed these knights to the sacred vows of poverty, chastity, and obedience (Barber 1993), as depicted in the Templar seal (see Figure 1).

Figure 1: The Templar seal showing two knights on one horse, believed to be Hugues de Payens and Godfrey de Saint-Omer

The seal, bearing an image of two knights riding a single horse, is more than a mere decorative motif, as it provides a window into the very essence of the Templar identity, a story that binds humility, unity, and duality. The esoteric narrative of this image is a nod to the humble economic circumstances of the Templars in their early years, when two knights would share a single horse during their travels. The seal served as a touchstone for their beginnings, a pictorial chronicle reminding them of their initial sacrifices and the principles of unity that bound them together. However, under the esoteric, the seal is a potent symbol that reveals deeper facets of the Templar ethos. The duality of the image, with two knights riding a solitary horse, encapsulates the dual roles of the Templars as warriors and monks. In addition to their seal, the Templars could be recognized by their distinctive white mantles marked with a red cross. The use of these "brand" images framed the multifarious Templar identity—a seamless blend of spiritual and military powers (Barber 1993). The order's motto was *Non nobis Domine, non nobis, sed nomini tua da gloriam* ("Not to us, O Lord, but to your name from 'glory'"). The motto comes from verses of Psalm 113 (ancient Vulgate) or of the incipit of Psalm 115 (according to Hebrew numbering; 114 of the Bible) (ibid.). The phrase signified their commitment to selflessness and the greater purpose they believed they served. It was later abandoned as they succumbed to pride and ostentation.

The Templars emerged against the backdrop of the Crusades, a time of fervent religious zeal and military conflict (ibid.). Their mission was one of both military and spiritual significance. Originally known as the "Poor Fellow-Soldiers of Christ and of the Temple of Solomon," they sought to safeguard the holy sites and ensure the safety of the faithful in the face of mounting threats from Muslim forces (ibid.). They became synonymous with the Crusader cause, their reputation as skilled warriors spreading far and wide. They engaged in numerous campaigns, fighting alongside other Christian forces against the Muslims in the Holy Land. Their strategic prowess and unwavering dedication earned them admiration and respect, solidifying their place as a formidable military order (ibid.).

As their ranks grew, the Templars gained recognition and support from influential figures, including Bernard of Clairvaux, who played a pivotal role in solidifying their status as an official religious order. Bernard was a French abbot known for revitalizing Benedictine monasticism through the Order of Cistercians. Coming from a noble family, he joined the Cistercian abbey at Cîteaux in 1113, later founding a new house at Clairvaux where he served as abbot. A prominent figure in ecclesiastical politics, Bernard played a vital role in the selection of Pope Innocent II and promoted the Second Crusade. He was canonized as a saint in 1174 (ibid.).

With the backing of the Bernard of Clairvaux and the Church, the Templars flourished. They were not merely warriors, but also administrators, overseeing vast estates and managing financial affairs for the Crusader states. Despite their notable acts of bravery, their dependence on alms led to such large donations that they broke their vow of poverty and expanded throughout Europe. From these donations and the subsequent acquisition of lands, castles, and treasures, the Templars developed an innovative system of banking and financial services that allowed them to amass considerable wealth and a network of support throughout Europe (ibid.). By the end of the twelfth century, they had grown rich and powerful. Their wealth became a topic of fascination and speculation, fueling rumors and conspiracy theories that persist to this day. Some say there is still Templar gold hidden throughout various parts of France and Portugal. Even the Nazis, particularly the *Schutzstaffel* (SS) under Heinrich Himmler, were engaged in extensive quests for multiple forms of occult power and artifacts, including the supposed lost treasures of the Knights Templar.

The Templars' financial success would also sow the seeds of their downfall, however, as envy and greed cast a shadow of suspicion upon them (ibid.) In addition to financial corruption, the Templars' once-glorious legacy was tarnished by accusations of heresy and secret rituals. Their rapid rise to power and their immense wealth drew the attention of powerful groups who saw an opportunity to seize their assets and eliminate a perceived threat.

The Assassins

Beneath the silhouetted minarets and sun-bleached walls of the ancient Near East, amidst a tableau of knights and castles, we find a tale of a tenuous alliance. In a twist of fate, two formidable orders of the medieval world and former archnemeses, the Knights Templar and the Assassins, found common ground. Like an ancient manuscript whose every page tells the tale of a complex web of alliances, religious conviction, and strategy, their story was shrouded in mystery. The name *Baphomet* may have originated in the shadowy alliances and diplomacy between these powerful groups, each as controversial as it was influential. Clues are spread out from the towering spires of European cathedrals to the fortress-studded hills of the Holy Land, rede-fining our understanding of medieval geopolitics and religious maneuvering. This is where we find the Assassins, a group with a different agenda yet uncannily similar methods to those of the Templars.

The Assassins were a radical group emerging from the Ismaili sect of Shia Islam during the Crusades. Known as the *Nizari Ismailis*, the Assassins were followers of Nizar ibn al-Mustansir, whom they revered as the rightful imam. Nizar ibn al-Mustansir was an important religious and political leader from the eleventh century who belonged to a branch of Islam called the Ismailis. He claimed to be the rightful ruler, or caliph, of a powerful Islamic dynasty called the Fatimids. However, there was a lot of disagreement about who should be the ruler, leading to a major split within the Ismaili community. The group that supported Nizar became known as the Nizari Ismailis and they continue to follow the line of leaders, or imams, descended from him even today. Its origins shrouded in debate, the name *Assassins* has long intrigued scholars, but it is believed to stem from the Arabic word *hashishin*, alluding to their alleged use of hashish (Lewis 2002).

The rise of the Assassins marked a significant chapter in history. Nestled amidst the remote mountain fortresses of Persia and Syria, the Assassins crafted a formidable power base. While they engaged in various endeavors, their tactics of political assassination gained them infamy. Often targeting military and political leaders from the dominant Sunni Islam, they strategically struck fear into the hearts of their adversaries. Their elite operatives, known as the *fida'i*, skillfully infiltrated enemy ranks, attacking at opportune moments with a potent combination of lethality and psychological manipulation. Foremost among the leaders of the Assassins was Hassan-i Sabbah, a figure who commanded reverence and fear alike. Establishing their stronghold at Alamut in northern Iran in 1090 CE, Sabbah and his disciples orchestrated a reign of influence that reverberated across the region, yet over time the Templars established states in regions surrounding Assassin strongholds as well (Tschudy 1776). For centuries, the Assassins wielded significant power, their order leaving an indelible mark on the pages of history. However, their supremacy met a formidable challenge in the middle of the thirteenth century, when the Mongols emerged as a relentless force, overpowering the Assassins and bringing an end to their reign.

The Templars and the Assassins had markedly different objectives and ideologies: the former sought to secure Christian control of holy sites in the Levant, while the latter wanted to carve out a state in the region for themselves that was free of both Sunni and Crusader control. Nevertheless, both groups shared enough similarities that they would eventually make an alliance of convenience. This led to diplomatic communications and treaties, one of which was well documented. In 1129, Count Hugh of Champagne visited the Assassin fortress at Alamut, perhaps leading to a truce between the two groups.

The parallels between the Templars and the Assassins begin with their shared adversary: the Sunni Seljuks. The Seljuks were a significant thorn in the sides of both factions, unifying them against a common enemy. Furthermore, both groups were branded as heretical and faced intense persecution from mainstream religious authorities, potentially fostering a unique bond or shared understanding based on their mutual struggles. They both maintained a covert, hierarchical structure that seemed to

mirror each other, indicative of similar organizational principles. Not only that, but they shared specific practices, such as the
construction of fortifications (strategic strongholds designed
for defense and control) and the use of religious indoctrination
as a tool to unify and motivate their respective members. The
striking similarities in their operations, practices, and challenges
suggest a deeper relationship than meets the eye; they hint at
the possibility of influence or an exchange of ideas between the
groups, perhaps even more than just a political alliance, which
would have offered them a chance to share knowledge and strat-
egies in the face of their common adversaries and struggles. The
belief that the Templars were influenced by Assassin doctrines
is fueled by the understanding that both groups were rumored
to possess secret knowledge, and the Templars were accused of
heresy based on practices that were similar to those ascribed to
the Assassins.

But while these points suggest possible interaction and
influence, they do not provide conclusive evidence of a sustained,
formal alliance. Critics of the Templar/Assassin theory argue
that these points merely reflect pragmatic political maneuvering and cultural exchange. Some scholars have argued that this
line of thinking is based in misconceptions and prejudices of
contemporary historians and does not indicate a deep or lasting
partnership between the Templars and Assassins. If the Templars and the Assassins were not allied, then what other evidence
could suggest that the Templars had been influenced by Islam?

While this mystery is over six hundred years old, it is important to remember that even in the Middle Ages, people had order
and structure to their everyday lives. It is a mistake to fall into
the trap of thinking that people "long ago" were so different

from us. Even the Sumerians, a civilization over six thousand years old, kept records and documented their lives in detail, including court cases. Likewise, there are many transcripts of the trials of the Templars from the fourteenth century. These historical documents have been preserved over the centuries and are housed in various archives, libraries, and historical collections around the world, including the Vatican Archives, the National Archives of France, the British Library, and the historical archives of several European countries where the Knights Templar lived (Spain, Portugal, Italy, and Germany). The records include interrogation transcripts, accusations and charges, confessions, and proceedings and judgments.

One of the charges made in these records was that the Templars had "renounced Christ and spat on the cross," which some have connected to the Assassins' alleged practice of *taqiyya* (Cook 2003). Taqiyya is a concept in Shia Islam that permits a person to deny their faith, to sin, or to commit acts against their faith under duress, threat, or persecution (ibid.). The term originates from the Arabic word meaning "prudence" or "fear," and is seen as a survival strategy that allows the faithful to protect themselves in the most hostile circumstances or under threat of persecution. This narrative suggests that during their interactions with the Assassins, the Templars may have been introduced to taqiyya, which they later adopted. Thus, when they were accused of spitting on the cross and renouncing Christ, their confession was not necessarily an indication of their true faith but rather a survival strategy borrowed from the Assassins. In this view, the Templars were not genuine heretics but instead were using religious dissimulation to protect themselves. This is often used as evidence of Assassin *influence* over the Templars rather than a diplomatic and political alliance of necessity.

The Knights' Fall

The story of the Templars' downfall contains evidence of conspiracy and betrayal. Whispers of clandestine rites and esoteric knowledge sent shockwaves through the corridors of power, striking fear into the hearts of those who saw the Templars' influence as a threat to their own (Barber 2012). As the Templars faced accusations of heresy and idol worship, the tendrils of suspicion tightened around the once-mighty order. Visions of an order corrupted by dark forces emerged, casting doubt upon their noble intentions and sparking a tempest of intrigue (Haag 2009). The stakes were high, and powerful figures conspired in the shadows, their actions threatening to bring the Templars to their knees (Read 2009). Interrogations turned into ordeals of unspeakable torture that extracted confessions and renunciations from once-proud defenders of the faith. The flames of persecution engulfed the Templars, testing their resolve and revealing the fragility of even the most steadfast souls (Haag 2009). Yet, amidst the torment, a few brave Knights stood defiant, steadfastly clinging to their integrity and righteousness, determined to face their fate with dignity (Read 2009).

As the thirteenth century neared its conclusion, the Templars had become the subject of suspicion and uncertainty both within the clergy and among the general public. Well known for their excessive indulgence in alcohol, the Templars were unfortunately associated with houses of disrepute. Rumors and allegations surrounding the order had reached Clement V even before he assumed the papacy in 1305. In a crucial turning point in the history of the Templars, King Philip IV of France, heavily indebted to the order and seeking to eliminate these financial obligations, initiated a ruthless campaign against them in 1307. This campaign was underpinned by a variety of serious charges against the Templars, including desecration of the cross and Christ during initiation, worshipping an idol, excluding words of consecration at Mass, granting absolution by lay leaders, and encouraging unnatural vice (Robinson 2009). Further investigations into these charges uncovered some startling practices. Some Templars confessed to venerating an idol resembling a cat, which could be red, gray, black, or spotted. As part of this unconventional ritual, the cat was sometimes kissed near its tail or coated with fat derived from roasted infants. Templar initiates were also allegedly compelled to consume food mixed with the cremated remains of their deceased comrades, a type of sorcery believed to impart the bravery of the departed knights to the living (ibid.).

Other accusations included the following (Nicholson 2011):

- Upon being initiated into the order, after taking the vow of obedience, new members were required to renounce Christ and disrespect the cross by spitting on it.

- They then kiss the Templar conducting the initiation on various intimate places.

- They occasionally worshipped a cat during their secret meetings.

- They engaged in inappropriate sexual activities.

- They worshipped idols in different provinces, which they believed enriched them and made flowers bloom and the earth sprout.
- They always wore a cord that had been rubbed against one of these idols, believing it offered protection.

Despite the nature of these charges, the admission ceremonies are widely accepted and seem truthful, making it difficult to dismiss them completely. For example, the denial of Christ was to be done three times, likely imitating Saint Peter's denial. This was perceived as a test of the pledge of obedience they had just taken to the order. All accused Templars argued that they acted under duress; they only verbally denied their faith without doing so in their hearts. When required to spit on the cross, they claimed to have deliberately missed it. In some instances, Templars who resisted these acts were threatened with severe consequences, scaring them into compliance. Some Templars recounted being so terrified that they forgot whether they performed these acts or not. Many were deeply upset and regretful about what they did, wishing they could reverse their actions even if it meant suffering physical harm.

Historian Michelet (1847/2011) offered a potential explanation of these initiation rituals in his *History of France*. He suggests that these ceremonies could be metaphorical, derived from the rites of the early Church. He proposes that the initiate was first portrayed as a sinner, following Peter's example of denying Christ. The initiate then symbolically expressed his sinful state by disrespecting the cross, after which he was metaphorically cleansed and admitted into a higher state of faith. One particularly controversial ritual was the kiss: according to the charges, the initiation required the novice to kiss the Templar performing the ceremony on the mouth, on the rear end, on the navel, and finally, on the penis (ibid.). Depositions from several Templars suggest that this was indeed true. (While not all elements were explicitly covered in the examinations, many of the rituals and practices attributed to the Templars are confirmed by multiple witnesses, affirming their authenticity.) Given the repugnant nature of this act to many, a gradual shift occurred to kissing only the *anca*, a medieval Latin term for the base of the spine. It seems the initiator had the discretion to waive this requirement if deemed appropriate. Bertrand de Somorens from the Amiens diocese recounts a ceremony where initiates were instructed to kiss the initiator's anus; however, they instead opted to lift his clothes and kiss his spine (ibid). Etienne de Dijon, a presbyter from the Langres diocese, shares that he was told to kiss the initiator's anus as per the order's custom, but this requirement was waived due to his status as a presbyter, or elder in the church hierarchy. Similarly, presbyter Pierre de Grumenil was excused from this act and allowed to kiss only the initiator's navel. Ado de Dompierre, another presbyter, was pardoned for the same reason, as were numerous others. A Templar named Pierre de Lanhiac narrates that, upon his initiation, he was asked to perform this act, but his uncle, who was also a member, successfully petitioned for him to be excused (ibid.).

Pope Clement V, under pressure from King Philip IV of France, reluctantly initiated an inquiry into these allegations. However, King Philip acted preemptively, arresting all Templars in France even before the investigation was completed. Prominent figures, such as Grand Master Jacques de Molay and the order's preceptors, found themselves under scrutiny. The inquiry was conducted in front of three cardinals, four public notaries, and several other respectable individuals. During these proceedings, Templars confessed to numerous transgressions, including the denial of Christ and spitting on the cross during their induction into the Templar order. Despite these damning confessions, Pope Clement V demonstrated restraint. Instead of condemning the entire order based on the infractions of the grand master and his closest brethren, he opted to commission a papal inquiry in Paris in November 1309 (Newman 2007). Overseeing the proceedings were ecclesiastical officials of the highest order. Despite a handful of knights, including the grand master himself, retracting their previous admissions, a storm of damning confessions persisted (Barber 2012). During a Templar trial in England, it is widely believed that the English king, Edward II, in a display of humanity, refrained from using torture due to his initial unwillingness to entertain any allegations against the order. This approach resulted in the Templars denying all charges initially, but after persuasion—including the possible use of torture—some confessed their guilt and were absolved. However, in France, the trials were conducted more stringently, resulting in the execution of fifty-four knights who had recanted their confessions. They were declared "relapsed heretics" and burned at the stake in 1310 (ibid.). In 1314, Grand Master Jacques de Molay met the same fate.

The accusations, confessions, and trials of the Templars marked a significant turning point in the order's history, leaving an enduring mark on their legacy. In each of the Templar trials, the courts employed varied techniques and yielded unique outcomes. While we cannot cover every trial of the Templars in this book, it is important to note that these events have given

historians clues with which to build their own cases about the
occult activities of the Templars. Historians who argue in favor
of the Templars typically emphasize two main points: the confessions were extracted under torture and are therefore discred-
itable, and the trials were a conspiracy between the king and the
pope aimed at acquiring the Templars' wealth. Are these the real
reason for the Templars' downfall, or the exoteric explanation
of the events that transpired? Either way, there is an esoteric
understanding in the dual nature of the Knights Templar. As
implied in the testimony of an English knight, Stephen de Sta-
pelbrugge, "there were two modes of reception, one lawful and
good and the other contrary to the Faith" (Castle 1907). Some
of the knights were privy to the order's secret doctrine, while
most were kept in the dark. Perhaps it is from this darkness that
Baphomet emerged.

Muhammad or Misunderstanding?

The Templars' alleged worship of Baphomet has been the subject of much speculation and controversy throughout the centuries. Some claim that Baphomet represents an esoteric deity
or a hidden aspect of Templar beliefs, symbolizing the pursuit
of hidden knowledge and spiritual enlightenment (Barber 1993).
Others argue that Baphomet was merely a fabrication used as
a tool by adversaries to tarnish the order's reputation (Barber
2012). To understand the significance of Baphomet within the
Templar context, we must explore its symbolism. Baphomet is
often depicted as a composite being, embodying both male and
female elements, representing the harmonization of opposites
(Lévi 1855/1896). Its symbolism extends beyond the material

realm, touching upon spiritual, philosophical, and occult dimensions (Partner 1990).

Through meticulous analysis of historical texts, artwork, and contemporary accounts, we seek to shed light on the intricate relationship between the Knights Templar and the figure of Baphomet. However, we must tread carefully as we navigate this confusion of historical accounts and conjectures. The limited primary sources and the inherent secrecy of the Templars make it challenging to separate fact from fiction. Moreover, as we explore this potential relationship between the Knights Templar and Baphomet, let's remember the context of these narratives. They stem from an era marked by misunderstandings and skewed perceptions, especially toward the Muslim world. Crusaders of the time often held a deep-seated prejudice against Muslims, seeing them as enemies to their cause. Likewise, the Muslims saw the Crusaders as invaders and enemies to *their* cause. This bias colored their actions, their beliefs, and the stories that have been passed down to us. It is our task to sift through these narratives with a keen awareness of these historical prejudices, seeking to understand the truth behind the myth.

The Templars' demise, marked by the suppression and persecution they faced, only further obscures the truth surrounding their alleged connection to Baphomet (Barber 1993). Some argue that Baphomet was revered as a sacred idol or deity by the Templars, serving as a focal point for their esoteric rituals and beliefs (Schonfield 1984). Others view the rumored connection as a fabrication concocted by the order's detractors to smear their reputation and hasten their downfall (Barber 2012). This dichotomy fits the symbol of Baphomet, depicted as a creature of dual nature, embodying masculine and feminine traits.

Baphomet symbolizes the unity of opposing forces and the pursuit of hidden wisdom (Lévi 1855/1896). Its esoteric significance extends beyond conventional religious boundaries, hinting at a deeper spiritual truth that the Templars may have sought to unveil (Partner 1990).

The once-esteemed Templars stood accused of worshipping an entity dubbed *Baphomet*. The mysterious figure was said to manifest as an idol in the shape of a head, according to the king's inquisitive officials. The term *baffomet*—which appears in the trial records, particularly those from southern France—adds another layer of mystery. It has been used to describe an image or idol resembling a bearded man, purported to symbolize Baphomet. Many accounts align with the idea that the Baphomet of the Templars was not an anthropomorphic goat, but rather a severed human head. According to the testimonies of Templars, the head seemed only to be displayed during select secret chapter meetings. Various Templars testified about its existence, with some even claiming to have seen it. Most described it as the size of a man's head, sporting a fierce face and usually a white beard. Descriptions varied, suggesting each Templar house may have had its own version of the idol. When the idol was presented, it was typically worshipped, and several Templars confessed to being terrified by its appearance. The idol's role and the Templars' relationship with it are still unknown, but some believe it might be connected to Eastern Gnostic ideologies.

According to one Templar's testimony upon joining the order, he was guided to a head on the chapel's altar that he was supposed to revere (see Figure 2). Although its size matched a human head, he was unable to describe it further, except for noting a reddish hue. Another Templar claimed to have witnessed the head on two occasions—once in Paris, adorned with a beard and being worshipped by the members, who referred to it as their savior (Wright 1966). Deodatus Jaffet, a Templar from southern France, recounted being shown a three-faced idol upon his initiation, with instructions to worship it as the savior of both himself and the order (ibid.). Guillaume de Arrablay, the king's almoner, talked of a silver head placed on the altar during his reception, worshipped by the chapter members. He believed it to be the head of one of the eleven thousand virgins until rumors after the order's arrest made him suspect it was the idol, with its dual faces, menacing appearance, and silver beard (ibid.).

Figure 2: Three men kneel on the steps of an altar and pray to an idol, a head with pointed ears and mane radiating out around a human face. Image courtesy of Universitätsbibliothek Heidelberg.

Scholars, such as those cited by Neugebauer-Wölk (2001) in the analysis of hermetic thinking in the Enlightenment, have pointed out that *baffomet* is a word borrowed from Provençal, a language once widely spoken in southern France. Referring to none other than the prophet Muhammad, the word was used to indicate an idol erroneously believed to be worshipped by Muslims. It was common during the Crusades to consider Islam as a form of heresy rather than a distinct religion. Some even brazenly insinuated that Muhammad was under the influence of Jews, heretics, and even diabolical forces, thereby feeding into the prejudices and misconceptions of the time. Misunderstandings and misrepresentations of Islam were unfortunately common-place (Neugebauer-Wölk 2001).

Templars, when confronted with allegations of idol worship, may have drawn upon familiar biblical narratives to describe their so-called idol. The descriptions offered depict small, golden figures, often perched atop columns. Some bear devilish features, such as horns and hooves, adding something more sinister to these allegations (ibid.). These historical charges and the term *Baffometus* were forgotten, languishing in obscurity for centuries until they were resurrected by Pierre Dupuy in the mid-seventeenth century. Dupuy, an eminent historian, unearthed these original documents and extensively quoted them in his 1654 book, subsequently republished several times. Further, scholar Friedrich Nicolai in his work *Versuch über die Beschuldigungen welche dem Tempelher-renorden gemacht worden, und über dessen Geheimni* (1782), altered the spelling from *Baffometus* to *Baphometus*, sparking renewed interest and opening up a Pandora's box of interpretations for this provocative figure.

Some knights from the south provided an additional detail about the idol. Gauserand de Montpesant from Provence mentioned an idol resembling Baffomet presented by his superior. Another, Raymond Rubei, referred to a wooden head with Baphomet's image, which he worshipped by kissing its feet and uttering "Yalla," a word borrowed from the Saracens. A Florentine Templar claimed that during the order's secret chapters, one brother showed the idol to another and said, "Adore this head—this head is your god and your Mahomet" (ibid.) During the Middle Ages, *Mahomet*, or Muhammad, was a term generally applied to an idol or false deity. Some scholars speculate that Baphomet might be a distortion of the word *Muhammad*, which would have sounded to them like "Mahomet," insinuating that the Templars may have covertly adopted Islam. However, a more compelling interpretation, notably from the orientalist Baron Joseph von Hammer-Purgstall, suggests that this word is related to certain art objects from the thirteenth century, decorated with various figures mainly composed of small statues, containers, and cups (Hammer-Purgstall 1818/2017); see Figure 3.

The potential connection between the Templars and the Gnostics, inferred from these obscure artifacts and inscriptions, spurred a wave of new research. Historians, theologians, and scholars from various fields aimed to understand if these two seemingly disparate groups indeed shared a common thread. According to Hammer-Purgstall, the Templars seemed to have adopted some form of Gnostic ritual practices, symbolism, or even metaphysical concepts (ibid.). While the exact translation of the formula inscribed on these artifacts remains somewhat elusive, it undeniably alludes to an esoteric tradition or belief system. Thus, the Templars' alleged adoption of such practices

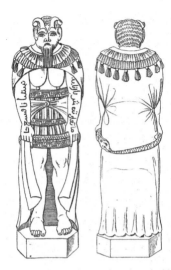

Figure 3: Illustration of a carved Templar artifact, described by later authors as a "Baphometic idol." Source: J. Hammer-Purgstall, Mysterium Baphometis Revelatum, *Tab I, Fig 7-8 (1818).*

suggests a radically different understanding of their faith than the orthodox Christianity they professed. Yet the confessions made under duress during the Inquisition and the hints found on these objects remain the main sources for such speculations. Inevitably, some scholars remained skeptical, raising questions about the authenticity of these confessions and the reliability of their interpretation. Nevertheless, the narrative put forth by Hammer-Purgstall offers a fascinating perspective on the secretive nature of the Templars. Whether or not they truly adopted Gnostic practices or maintained a parallel esoteric belief system, these findings shed light on the possibility of diverse spiritual beliefs coexisting, and possibly even converging, during the Middle Ages. This paints a more complex and nuanced picture of religious and philosophical diversity during this period, opening the door for further exploration of the beliefs and practices in Medieval Europe.

While the idea that Baphomet is a misunderstood Muhammad is plausible, it is important to avoid jumping to conclusions. Historical records from the Templars' time are limited, broken up, and sometimes biased. The information we do have comes from sources that might have had their own political, religious, or personal reasons for saying what they did, which makes us question how reliable they are. In light of these considerations, it is prudent to approach the theory of Baphomet as a mispronunciation with a healthy dose of skepticism. While linguistic misunderstandings were undoubtedly a feature of medieval encounters, we must remain cautious in extrapolating this theory to explain the Templars' alleged worship of Baphomet. The quest for understanding the true nature of the Templar–Baphomet connection necessitates a comprehensive examination of historical records, primary sources, and comparative religious studies. It is an exploration that invites us to delve beyond linguistic speculations and seek a more profound conclusion. Indeed, the realm of linguistic interpretations surrounding the term *Baphomet* is not limited to the Muhammad mispronunciation theory. There are other intriguing possibilities that have been proposed, adding further layers of complexity to the mysterious origins of the word *Baphomet*.

One alternative interpretation suggests that *Baphomet* may be derived from the Greek words *baphe* and *metis*, which together allude to baptism and wisdom (Barber 2012). The Greek word for wisdom and the symbolism of seven archons both align with known elements of Gnostic tradition. Gnostic doctrines were known to incorporate elements from various traditions, including Christianity, Judaism, Greek philosophy, and even Eastern mysticism. They generally espoused a dualistic world-view regarding the material world as fundamentally evil and the spiritual world as inherently good. In Gnostic belief systems, wisdom or knowledge was a divine spark trapped within the material confines of the human body, yearning to be released to rejoin the divine realm. This interpretation ties into the Templars' initiation rituals and their quest for esoteric knowledge, implying a deeper symbolic meaning.

Another linguistic avenue of exploration involves the Old French term *bafometz*, which appeared in certain medieval texts and could have influenced the development of the term *Baphomet* (Ralls 2003). The etymology and precise meaning of *bafometz* remain uncertain, but it highlights the linguistic complexities and potential sources of inspiration for the creation of the Baphomet concept. Still another theory relies on the work of Émile Littré, in his *Dictionnaire de la langue francaise* (1877). Littré proposed a cabalistic explanation of the word. This involved reversing the abbreviation "tem. o. h. p. ab," which stands for *templi omnium hominum pacis abbas*, meaning "abbot" or "father of the temple of peace of all men." Littré attributes this information to the "Abbé Constant," who in reality is Alphonse-Louis Constant, better known by the pseudonym Éliphas Lévi, a central figure in the evolution of the Baphomet icon whom we will discuss in depth in Chapter 3.

Again, it is essential to approach these linguistic interpretations with caution and acknowledge the challenges inherent in deciphering the true origins and intended meaning of a term that has been shrouded in mystery for centuries. Without definitive historical evidence or a unanimous consensus among scholars, these alternative linguistic theories remain speculative and subject to ongoing scholarly debate. Therefore, while the Muhammad mispronunciation theory and other linguistic interpretations offer intriguing possibilities, they should be considered as speculative avenues of exploration rather than conclusive explanations. The true meaning and significance of the term *Baphomet* within the context of the Templars' alleged worship continue to elude us, prompting us to dig further into the historical records, symbology, and cultural milieu of the time in our quest for understanding.

Symbolic Significance

The Templars were known to possess a deep understanding of ancient mystical teachings, drawing inspiration from various esoteric traditions. Baphomet, as a symbol, represented the culmination of their knowledge and spiritual practices. It embodied the synthesis of diverse spiritual concepts, blending elements from Gnosticism, Hermeticism, and other mystical traditions. Through the study of sacred geometry, alchemy, and ritual magic, the Templars, some believe, sought to uncover the secrets of the universe and the mysteries of divine wisdom. Baphomet may have served as a focal point for their esoteric explorations, representing the interplay between opposing forces, the balance of masculine and feminine energies, and the transcendence of duality.

For the Templars, Baphomet was not merely a symbol confined to the material realm but a doorway to the divine. Within the symbol of Baphomet, whatever it may have been to them, the Templars found a conduit to connect with the spiritual realms and attain higher states of consciousness. Through meditation, ritual practices, and devotion to Baphomet, they aimed to transcend the limitations of the physical world and attain spiritual enlightenment. Baphomet represented a union of the earthly and the divine, a harmonious fusion of the spiritual and the material. It symbolized the journey of the individual soul, seeking to transcend the mundane and ascend to higher planes of existence. The Templars seemed to believe that by communing with Baphomet, they could awaken the dormant aspects of their own divine nature and unlock the pathways to spiritual revelation.

The absence of a concrete visual representation of Baphomet left by the Knights Templar poses a challenge in our quest to understand its symbolism fully. Unlike many other symbols associated with historical figures or organizations, the Templars did not leave behind a definitive image or depiction of Baphomet. Instead, we are left to piece together fragments of information from various historical sources, accounts, and interpretations. One reported artifact left behind was found in a museum owned by the Duc de Blacas: a rectangular box, made of limestone, from Burgundy. The box's lid features a carved figure, nude, wearing a headdress like Cybele, an ancient deity. The figure is holding up chains—symbols linked to Gnostic beliefs according to Hammer-Purgstall—and is surrounded by celestial symbols. Sculpted scenes on the sides show various cryptic ceremonies. The artifact was part of a collection that included another similar box, this one from Tuscany, and a marble bowl from Vienna's imperial museum. These artifacts featured related imagery and themes. For instance, one showed an odd figure on an eagle with the sun and moon symbols. Hammer-Purgstall speculated that these artifacts might have been used in secretive rituals, possibly by the Templars, a theory he found plausible considering that symbols found on these objects were mentioned in some Templar confessions. Most artifacts featured inscriptions in Arabic, Greek, and Roman characters. Hammer-Purgstall believed that these inscriptions, which were mostly proper names and religious formulas, were copied from an Eastern original by a European who didn't fully understand the text. He proposed that the word *Baphomet* came from the Greek words for "baptism of wisdom" and was associated with Gnostic sects in the East. Furthermore, he connected the iconography on these artifacts with statements from Templar trials, such as the worship of a deity for its ability to make trees flourish and the earth germinate.

The multifaceted nature of Baphomet extends beyond its physical representation, encompassing deeper mystical meanings. Regardless of the actual form Baphomet took, the Templars saw Baphomet as a guide, a symbol that provided profound insights into the nature of reality and the divine in their pursuit of mystical truths. It was a reflection of their esoteric knowledge, their spiritual aspirations, and their devotion to uncovering the mysteries of existence. While we may lack direct visual evidence of what the Baphomet of the Templars looked like, the work of influential figures like Éliphas Lévi can offer valuable insights into the symbolic analysis of Baphomet. Lévi's influential book *Transcendental Magic, Its Doctrine and Ritual* serves as a crucial resource in our exploration of Baphomet's meaning and significance. His description and symbolic interpretation of Baphomet fill in some of the gaps left by historical sources, offering a framework for deeper analysis. While we must approach Lévi's account with a critical eye and recognize that it is one interpretation among many, his work offers a valuable framework for understanding the symbolic complexity of Baphomet. Through a careful analysis of Lévi's writings and an exploration of other relevant sources, we will strive to uncover the hidden truths and illuminate the intricate symbolism of Baphomet. In Chapter 3, we will do a deeper analysis of Lévi's account and examine the intricate symbolism and hidden meanings he attributed to Baphomet. By integrating Lévi's insights with our examination of historical sources, we aim to paint a comprehensive and nuanced picture of Baphomet's significance within the context of the Templars' beliefs and practices. But first, we must leave behind the realm of the Knights Templar and venture into the shadowed world of Gnostic traditions, where wisdom and esoteric knowledge converge.

Chapter 2

THE SOPHIA CONNECTION
Baphomet, the Gnostics, and Pathways of Knowledge

Those who have been perfected are given
their teachings in secret, by means of symbols.

—CLEMENT OF ALEXANDRIA,
Early Christian theologian (150 CE–215 CE)

Gnosticism, a term laden with complexity and intrigue, has long been a lodestar in the nocturnal sky of Western esoteric thought. This ancient yet evergreen branch of spiritual tradition has captivated the intellectual and mystical appetites of figures as diverse as the alchemical sage Paracelsus and the twentieth-century occultist Aleister Crowley. It is a term that embodies an eternal yearning for hidden knowledge, a desire to pierce the veil between the visible and the invisible realms. While the twentieth-century discovery of texts like the Nag Hammadi library has shed new light on this arcane tradition, a sense of mystery still lingers. Much like a puzzle that reveals a different picture with each assembly, Gnosticism eludes monolithic interpretation. The intricate interplay between theology and ecclesiastical politics that characterized its inception has rendered it a versatile term—often serving as a catch-all designation for heretical thought, a notion conceived in the crucible of theological struggle and ecclesiastical censure.

During the intellectual and spiritual fervor of the nineteenth and early twentieth centuries, scholars and mystics alike dived into the maze of ancient Gnostic teachings. Yet what they found was far from a straightforward elucidation; instead, they encountered a web of metaphysical intricacies, a maze rich in symbolism, esotericism, and allegory. Moreover, Gnosticism's subterranean roots seemed to stretch far and wide, entangled with various traditions such as the Cathars, the Templars, and later, the occult revival that swept across a Europe undergoing sociopolitical upheaval. Gnosticism thus serves as an expansive backdrop against which a multitude of narratives can be depicted, from the feminist interpretations of the divine feminine to the intersection of Eastern and Western esoteric traditions.

This chapter will navigate this shadowy path, exploring the myriad ways in which Gnostic thought has been appropriated, interpreted, and reinvigorated throughout the ages. We will delve into figures like Sophia and Baphomet—archetypal embodiments of wisdom and duality, both compelling and controversial. These figures serve as guideposts in our journey through the complex interconnections of mysticism, sociopolitical landscapes, and the persistent human quest for transcendence. From the mystical doctrines of the Cathars and Templars—both subjects of theological persecution—to the tumultuous socioeconomic conditions that gave rise to the occult revival and the fascinating character of Éliphas Lévi, we will traverse centuries and ideologies. Ahead lies a journey through time, philosophy, and the many facets of hidden wisdom that have intrigued the human mind for millennia.

Sophia and Baphomet

The archetypal figures of Sophia and Baphomet reveal contrasting yet complementary facets of wisdom that transcend the limitations of worldly understanding. In these figures, we see two distinct yet converging pathways to transcendent wisdom.

Sophia, emerging from the complex matrix of Gnostic tradition, serves as an archetype of divine wisdom and the eternal feminine (see Figure 4). The texts that preserve her myths—such as the *Pistis Sophia*, the *Gospel of Philip*, and the *Hypostasis of the Archons*—present her not as a passive receptor of wisdom but as an active force engaged in the creation, dissolution, and transformation of worlds (Mead 2005; King 2003). She embodies the eternal quest for divine understanding and the pitfalls and triumphs that accompany it. Sophia's cosmic misstep is, in essence, a courageous act of striving to know the unknowable, a cautionary yet inspirational tale about the risks and rewards of seeking the ultimate truth (Pagels 1989).

In stark contrast, yet equally compelling, is Baphomet—a figure that eludes easy categorization. Unlike Sophia, Baphomet is less anchored in textual tradition and more a composite of iconographies, interpretations, and purposes. While Sophia serves as a clarion call to transcend material limitations and unite with the divine, Baphomet invites us to delve into the depths of earthly wisdom and engage with the more immanent, less abstract aspects of existence. In the realm of alchemy, Baphomet emerges as a potent symbol of transformation, reflecting the alchemist's goal to transmute base materials into higher forms, symbolic of spiritual elevation (Principe 2015). This wisdom is of a different quality but no less significant; it challenges us to find divinity not in lofty heavens but in the palpable materiality of the world.

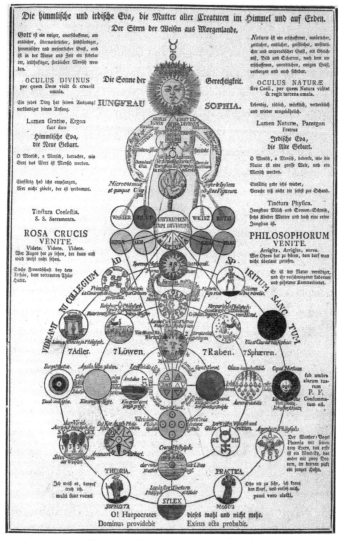

Figure 4: A mystical depiction of Sophia. Source: H. Madathanus Theosophus,
Geheime Figuren Der Rosenkreuzer, aus dem 16ten und 17ten
Jahrhundert *[The Secret Symbols of the Rosicrucians of the 16th and 17th
Centuries] (Altona, Germany, 1785).*

The differences between Sophia and Baphomet can be most vividly understood in the scopes of their transformative roles. Sophia's divine wisdom facilitates the soul's journey through the rays of cosmic complexities, guiding the inquisitive spirit toward the *pleroma* (fullness), where the broken fragments of divine light can reintegrate into wholeness (King 2003). Conversely, Baphomet's wisdom, though rooted in material reality, is no less enlightening. It calls for an alchemical transformation, not of the soul aspiring for heavenly ascent but of the very substance of earthly life aspiring for balance and integration (Hanegraaff 1997). There are resonances here with Jungian conceptions of individuation, where the Self evolves through the integration of opposites. Sophia and Baphomet can be seen as dual aspects of a cosmic drama unfolding both within and outside human consciousness (von Franz 1997). They are not disparate but complementary, each providing what the other lacks. Sophia, in her eternal quest for understanding, loses herself and finds herself, a narrative arc offering humanity a mythic template for spiritual progress. Baphomet, in its manifold forms and interpretations, teaches us to embrace complexity, contradiction, and the murky realms of the subconscious as avenues to wholeness.

The dialectic between Sophia's transcendent wisdom and Baphomet's immanent wisdom echoes through history, reverberating in different cultural epochs and finding novel expressions. From Gnostic cosmologies to alchemical manuscripts, from Cathar heresies to the modern occult revival, their archetypal energies persist, adapt, and inform diverse quests for wisdom, whether spiritual or material. These twin currents of wisdom—divine and earthly—merge most profoundly in the shadowy realms of the occult, where figures like Éliphas Lévi draw upon

both traditions to articulate a unified vision of human potential and cosmic order (Lévi 1855/1896). Through the lens of Lévi's
writings, both Sophia and Baphomet acquire new significances
and implications, their characteristics and energies intermingling
in a grand narrative that transcends their individual mythologies
and offers humanity a panoramic view of the manifold possibilities for achieving wisdom.

Sophia was vital personification to many Gnostics, but
especially the Cathars. They, too, sought a higher understanding that transcended orthodox religious limitations, and like
the Templars—often suspected of harboring secret Gnostic or
even "heretical" beliefs—the Cathars were a subject of ecclesiastical scrutiny and persecution. Their theology and cosmology
embraced dualistic principles and emphasized direct personal
experience of the divine, much like what we find in the symbols
of Sophia and Baphomet. It is in the landscape of Cathar spirituality that our quest to understand these ancient archetypes
takes its next intriguing turn.

The Cathars and the Templars

The Cathars, who emerged in the eleventh and twelfth centuries primarily in the Languedoc region of southern France,
constitute a compelling chapter in the history of religious and
esoteric thought. They were part of a broader Christian dualist
or Gnostic revival movement, much like their spiritual ances-
tors, the Bogomils of the Balkans (Lambert 1998). As inheritors
and practitioners of a form of Gnosticism, the Cathars offered
a spiritual worldview that stood in stark contrast to the prevailing dogmas of the Roman Catholic Church. Central to Cathar

belief was a form of dualism positing that the material world was the creation of a malevolent deity or Demiurge. This world was in contrast to a realm of pure spirit, overseen by a benevolent, transcendent God (Moore 2014). This dualistic worldview resonates strongly with earlier Gnostic conceptions, including the myth of Sophia, who, in her descent and struggle with the material world, represents the soul's journey toward liberation (Hoeller 2002). The Cathars also viewed human souls—much like the Gnostic Sophia—as divine sparks ensnared in a physical, earthly prison, under the dominion of the Demiurge. Their concept of liberation revolved around the purification of these entrapped souls, which was accomplished chiefly through a ritual known as the *Consolamentum* (O'Shea 2000). Administered to the "Perfects," or Parfaits, who had undergone rigorous moral and ascetic training, this ceremony was believed to cleanse the soul of its attachments to the material world and facilitate its return to the divine realm.

One cannot discuss the Cathars without mentioning the Albigensian Crusade, a brutal military campaign initiated by Pope Innocent III, aimed at exterminating Catharism in southern France (see Figure 5). Lasting from 1209 CE to 1229 CE, this crusade led to the deaths of thousands, including many innocent civilians, and resulted in the near-total eradication of the Cathar faith. Despite their tragic end, the legacy of the Cathars survived, capturing the imaginations of later esoteric and mystical traditions. The suppression of the Cathars, much like that of the Knights Templar, who were also accused of heresy and suppressed in the early fourteenth century, evinces the Church's often violent intolerance toward alternative spiritual paths (Barber 1993). Both groups, in their quests for a transcendent wisdom, rose above the doctrinal limitations imposed by the orthodoxy of their times. This invites speculation on potential points of ideological crossover between these two groups, particularly considering that the Templars had a presence in regions where Catharism was prevalent (ibid.).

The Cathars and the Templars were on similar quests for esoteric wisdom, albeit in disparate epochs and from differing theological standpoints. The Cathars, with their Gnostic influences, sought an ascendant spiritual realm far removed from

Figure 5: Expulsion of the Cathar inhabitants from Carcassonne in 1209. Source: Grandes Chroniques de France, British Library (1415).

the material world they saw as corrupted. Similarly, the Templars were reputed to have been keepers of arcane knowledge, potentially Gnostic or Kabbalistic in nature, as evidenced by the legends surrounding their mysterious figure of Baphomet. Both groups were the object of persecution, their beliefs leading them afoul of prevailing religious orthodoxy and thus casting them into the realm of the heretical (Barber 1993; Moore 2014). The symbology associated with the Cathars and Templars adds a layer of complexity to their legacies. The Cathars often used the dove as a symbol for the Holy Spirit, analogous to the Gnostic figure of Sophia as the embodiment of wisdom (Hoeller 2002). Their dualistic beliefs, ascetic practices, and tragic history form an intriguing parallel to the explorations of wisdom in different religious and esoteric traditions, serving as yet another chapter in humanity's ongoing quest to understand the transcendent.

The Occult Revival

Fast-forward to the late nineteenth century, and we find the Occult Revival emanating from a similar source of spiritual discontent. The Theosophists, Hermeticists, and assorted other esotericists of this era were disenchanted with the spiritual aridity they saw in their contemporary religious institutions. Just like the Cathars and Templars, they sought wisdom in ancient traditions and mystical experiences. However, their quest was given urgency by the seismic shifts occurring in the socioeconomic landscape, an intricate interplay of various intellectual, cultural, and economic forces. By the late nineteenth and early twentieth centuries, the Industrial Revolution had radically altered the face of society. Urbanization was rapidly expanding, pulling people away from rural areas and traditional community structures and creating both social dislocation and novel opportunities for cultural exchange.

This period was also marked by profound scientific advancements that threw into question conventional religious and philosophical worldviews. Charles Darwin's theory of evolution presented serious challenges to biblical literalism, while breakthroughs in psychology, particularly the work of Sigmund Freud and Carl Jung, pushed the boundaries of human understanding of the mind and spirit (Ellenberger 1981; Owen 2004). Meanwhile, anthropology was exposing Western culture to a myriad of religious and philosophical practices from around the world, amplifying an already present but latent desire to explore non-orthodox religious experiences (Stocking 1987). The rise of a prosperous middle class also created a fertile ground for the Occult Revival: this newly affluent segment of society had both the leisure time and the financial resources to explore alternative religious practices, purchase esoteric literature, and even travel to foreign countries in search of mystical wisdom. Additionally, the burgeoning printing press made it easier to widely circulate occult literature and correspondence courses, thus democratizing access to previously secretive traditions (McIntosh 2011). Politically, the era was marked by both optimism and anxiety. While there was strong faith in progress and human potential, political tensions and the forebodings of world wars contributed to a sense of societal unease. Many found in occultism an avenue for personal and societal transformation that stood apart from the crumbling pillars of established religion and the often-disheartening developments in politics and international affairs (Nelson 1969).

The Occult Revival, then, can be viewed as a reaction to and product of its times—a spiritual countercurrent to the disorienting transformations of the industrial age. Individuals found themselves living in a world increasingly defined by scientific rationalism and socioeconomic upheaval, and many sought a more integrated worldview that could reconcile the spiritual with the scientific. This desire often led them to resurrect or adapt older traditions, such as those represented by the Cathars and Templars, as they navigated the uncertain terrain of a rapidly evolving world (Hanegraaff 1997). In essence, the Occult Revival emerged as an attempt to navigate and make sense of a world undergoing tectonic shifts in virtually every area of human life. It offered a spiritual alternative to the orthodoxies that seemed unable to speak to the complexities and anxieties of a new age, serving as both a symptom and a response to the broader socioeconomic transformations that defined the era.

In the eclectic practices and teachings of the Occult Revival, we find the influence and even direct study of Cathar and Templar traditions. Theosophists and Hermeticists revived Gnostic and Kabbalistic lore, recognizing in them the same core yearning for spiritual ascension and transformative wisdom. Éliphas Lévi, one of the intellectual catalysts of the Occult Revival, illustrated this when he amalgamated the images of Baphomet and the tarot into a new esoteric paradigm. He effectively wove the Templar tradition into the history and legend of modern occultism, emphasizing its timeless quest for hidden wisdom (Lévi 1861).

The Cathars and Templars were intellectual and spiritual forerunners of the Occult Revival. They set the stage for a new generation of spiritual seekers, who, endowed with the freedom to synthesize a vast array of esoteric traditions, continued to quest for the same transcendent wisdom that has lured humanity for millennia. In a sense, the Occult Revival represents a maturation and expansion of the same esoteric impulses that fueled the Cathars and Templars—impulses that continue to resonate in today's spiritual landscape (Holroyd 1994). This interconnectedness suggests that the quest for transcendent wisdom is not confined to a particular time or place. Rather, it is a recurrent motif in the human story—a ceaseless quest that finds new expression in each epoch, yet is invariably linked to its predecessors.

Pioneers of Esoteric Feminism

The prevailing spiritual doctrines of the Middle Ages often relegated women to the periphery of religious and intellectual life. Against this backdrop, the Cathar and Templar orders stood as beacons of relative gender egalitarianism, illuminating pathways that later esoteric figures like Lévi would tread. The Cathar belief system incorporated a sophisticated cosmology where divine principles were not confined to masculine archetypes. Adept at syncretizing ideas, the Cathars held the notion of a dual God—both good and evil, masculine and feminine (Moore 2014). This idea diverged sharply from Catholic orthodoxy and provided theological ground for women to assume important religious roles. Notably, women could become *Parfaites*, the female equivalent of the Parfaits, taking on spiritual duties such as administering the Consolamentum, the Cathar rite of absolution (Costen 1997). Additionally, the Knights Templar are often painted with broad strokes that focus on their militaristic exploits, yet the code of chivalry they adhered to had a spiritual dimension deeply influenced by the Marian cult. The reverence for the Virgin Mary normalized the veneration of the feminine, both symbolically and practically (Barber 1993). Though women were not knights, they could be associated with the Templars in supportive roles and as benefactors (Nicholson 2011). This broadened the social space within which women could operate, presenting them as essential contributors to the Templar mission.

It is in the overlap between the Cathars and Templars that we find intriguing resonances with Lévi's later doctrines. Lévi was adamant about the essential equality between men and women, both in social and esoteric contexts (Lévi 1861). His construction of Baphomet incorporated both masculine and feminine elements, a symbiosis that hinted at divine completeness and could be seen as a conceptual heir to the dual God of the Cathars and the Marian veneration among the Templars (Lévi 1855/1896). The egalitarian threads woven into the fabric of the Cathar and Templar traditions were not lost to time. In fact, they can be seen as pioneering forms of esoteric feminism that laid the ground for later figures like Lévi, who saw in the balanced union of masculine and feminine a key to higher wisdom. This idea has had lingering effects, influencing later esoteric orders that champion gender inclusivity as a matter of spiritual principle (King 2003). The inclusion and, in some instances, elevation of women in Cathar and Templar belief systems demonstrate an undercurrent of resistance against the gender norms of their respective eras. These heterodox positions reverberate in the works of later esoteric thinkers like Lévi, who himself was deeply influenced by these Western mystical traditions.

Cross-Cultural Mysticism

The narrative of the Templars is often intertwined with their role as Christian warriors, defending the faith against infidels during the Crusades. However, to understand them purely in the context of religious conflict would be a gross simplification, as Chapter 1 explored. In reality, the Templars were not just warriors but also liaisons between Eastern and Western cultures. Their military presence in the Holy Land provided a unique vantage point from which they could absorb diverse religious and mystical teachings, and the evidence supporting such cross-cultural exchanges is indeed compelling.

One must mention their inevitable interaction with Islamic cultures before discussing the Templars in the Middle East. Some scholars suggest that the Templars had contact with Sufi orders, which were themselves an amalgamation of Islamic jurisprudence and mystical, esoteric wisdom (Mack 2001); see Figure 6. The Sufi concept of divine love, a notion that transcends the material world to seek unity with the divine, is strikingly reminiscent of the Templars' chivalric ideals. The Templars and Sufis shared an obsession with purification—be it of the soul or of the Holy Land (Upton 2001). Another point of intersection between the Templars and Eastern traditions lies in the realm of Jewish mysticism, specifically Kabbalah. Documents such as the Zohar provide glimpses into the inner workings of divine mechanics, akin to how the Templars viewed their quest for the Holy Grail (Scholem 1941). Although direct evidence linking the Templars with Kabbalistic learning is scant, the similarities in their conceptual frameworks—such as the focus on divine geometry and numerology—are difficult to ignore (Rankin 2010).

Figure 6: A Guler painting showing an imaginary meeting of Sufi saints (Baba Farid, Khawaja Qutub-ud-din, Hazrat Muin-ud-Din, Hazrat Dastgir, Abn Ali Kalandar, and Khawaja Nizamuddin Aulia); date unknown

Beyond Islamic and Jewish mysticism, there are intriguing suggestions that Templars were exposed to even more distant Eastern philosophies, possibly through the Silk Road or via Islamic scholars who had translated Hindu and Buddhist texts (Potts 1991). As noted in Chapter 1, some have interpreted the Templar seal depicting two knights on a single horse as symbolic

of duality, akin to the Eastern yin and yang, though this interpretation remains speculative (Partner 1990). The confluence of
these diverse traditions finds a unique expression in the realm
of alchemy. Much like the Sufi alchemists, Kabbalists, and Eastern philosophers, the Templars seemed to espouse a worldview
where the transformation of the material world into a divine
one was not just possible but mandated. Their quest for the
Holy Grail, often interpreted as an allegorical pursuit of divine
wisdom, appears to be an occidental reflection of these oriental
philosophies (Coudert 1999).

The echoes of Eastern thought acquired by the Templars
can be heard throughout Western esotericism. Later figures,
like Lévi, would inherit a tradition rich in the syncretism
of Eastern and Western mystical philosophies. Lévi's inclu-
sive esoteric vision, which borrowed elements from Kabbalah, alchemy, and Gnostic Christianity, is a testament to
the hybrid mystical landscape fertilized by the Templars (Lévi
1861). Although often misunderstood as mere crusading zeal-
ots, the Templars were actually a complex organization at the
crossroads of multiple civilizations. The evidence points to a
rich exchange of mystical wisdom between the Templars and
various Eastern traditions—ranging from Islamic Sufism and
Jewish Kabbalah to philosophies that originated even farther
East. Their influence has had a lasting impact, enriching the
Western esoteric tradition and paving the way for later figures
like Lévi to bring these strands together into a more comprehensive spiritual worldview. This is particularly true thanks to
the Golden Age of Islam, which would lay the foundation for
the rediscovery of these ancient wisdom traditions in the later
Italian Renaissance.

Resurgence of Ancient Wisdom

The Renaissance, with its reverberation through art, philosophy, and spiritual practices, was not an isolated event but
rather a culmination of various traditions and beliefs, among
which were the echoes of Catharism and Templar ideologies.
While both of these traditions emerged in the Middle Ages,
a period often denigrated as the so-called Dark Ages, their
philosophies found renewed interest and application during
the Renaissance.

Catharism, with its dualistic interpretation of good and
evil, matter and spirit, found a companion in the burgeoning
Renaissance philosophy of Neoplatonism. Pioneered by thinkers like Plotinus and revitalized by Renaissance luminaries such
as Marsilio Ficino, Neoplatonism also entertained a dualistic
worldview, differentiating the material world from the world of
forms, or ideal realities (Ficino 2004). Like the Cathars, Neoplatonists sought to transcend the material world through intellectual and spiritual practices, offering a path to enlightenment and
unity with the divine. Hermeticism, another prominent philosophical strand during the Renaissance, originated in ancient
Egypt but enjoyed a revival thanks to the translation of texts
like the *Corpus Hermeticum*. The Hermetic tradition focused on
alchemical transmutations and the reconciliation of opposites,
echoing the Templars' preoccupation with sacred geometry,
numerology, and mystical wisdom (Yates 1964). The Templars'
rumored association with the alchemical transformation—
turning base metal into gold or, more esoterically, elevating the
human soul—found resonance in the Hermetic tradition, which
also emphasized the possibility of transforming the "base" into

the "divine" (Principe 2015). Through the lens of history, the philosophies of the Cathars and Templars underwent not just continuation but also expansion and reinterpretation in the intellectual milieu of the Renaissance. This confluence of ideologies and beliefs endured and evolved, etching its imprint on the transformative epoch that would shape the future of Western magic.

As noted, both Catharism and Templar ideologies had Gnostic undertones—perceptions of a hidden, esoteric knowledge reserved for the initiated. Renaissance thinkers openly embraced the idea of hidden wisdom; for example, Giovanni Pico della Mirandola's famous *Oration on the Dignity of Man* celebrated human potential for divine ascension, which can be viewed as a continuation of Cathar and Templar philosophies on spiritual elevation (Pico della Mirandola 1486). The political and social climate of the Renaissance—characterized by the breakdown of feudal structures, the rise of humanism, and the challenges to ecclesiastical authority—provided fertile ground for the spread of Cathar and Templar ideas. Just as these medieval orders had been a response to the social and spiritual crises of their times, so too did Renaissance men and women find in Cathar and Templar ideologies answers to the uncertainties of a rapidly changing world.

Magick of the Renaissance

The Renaissance, often viewed as an age of rationalism and scientific awakening, also fostered a deep fascination with the mystical, magical, and esoteric. As Europe emerged from the shackles of the medieval period, it saw not only a revival of classical philosophy and art but also a renewed interest in occult practices and mystical symbolism. This fervor found expression in multiple domains—from alchemical treatises to emblematic artwork—and provides a rich foundation to explore our recurring themes of Baphomet, duality, and the confluence of religious and philosophical ideologies.

In the alchemical laboratories of the Renaissance, Baphomet found a symbolically congenial environment. Alchemy was a precursor to modern chemistry but steeped in mysticism. Alchemists like Heinrich Cornelius Agrippa and Paracelsus were interested in the transformation of base metals into gold—a metaphor for spiritual purification (Agrippa 1532). The depiction of Baphomet as an androgynous reconciler of opposites resonated with the alchemical aim of achieving the *Magnum Opus*, or the Great Work, of unifying dichotomies (Jung 1964). Ficino, a key figure in the Renaissance Neoplatonic revival, was instrumental in introducing the term *magick* into philosophical discourse. His work was infused with dualistic themes. For Ficino, magick was a way to comprehend the divine mysteries of the cosmos, using symbols as intermediaries (Ficino 2004). In this light, Baphomet could be seen as a powerful magickal symbol encompassing the dual aspects of material and spiritual, masculine and feminine, and drawing upon the same energies that Neoplatonists believed animated the universe.

The Hermetic tradition was another facet of Renaissance thought where the idea of duality played a significant role (Yates 1964). The Hermetic worldview advocated the concept of "as above, so below," echoing the Baphometic representation of uniting the heavenly and earthly realms. This Hermetic maxim profoundly influenced Renaissance magicians, who saw

the correspondence between celestial and terrestrial phenomena as evidence for a unified, albeit dualistic, universe (Principe
2015). The Renaissance art world also reflects this fascination
with mystical themes and duality. Leonardo da Vinci's *Vitruvian
Man* (see Figure 7) can be interpreted as a symbol of the duality of human existence—earthly and divine—just as Baphomet
embodies a myriad of dualities (Da Vinci 1490). The image of
the androgynous, angelic beings in his artwork speaks to the
period's preoccupation with reconciling opposites within a harmonious cosmic order.

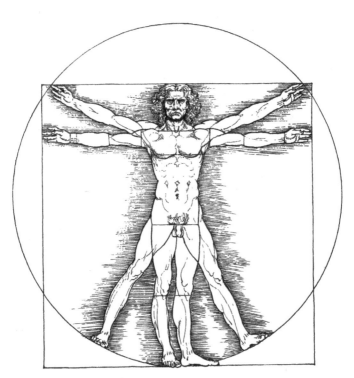

Figure 7: Da Vinci's Vitruvian Man, *ca. 1490*

Post-Enlightenment

The nineteenth century was a tumultuous time in France and much of Europe. The Industrial Revolution was in full swing, drastically altering the social fabric. While factories and industry offered unprecedented material advancements, they also created new social tensions. The division between the wealthy bourgeoisie and the struggling working class was widening, manifesting in various ways including social unrest, strikes, and even revolutions. It was during this period of upheaval that one of the greatest occultists, Éliphas Lévi, found himself at the nexus of these sweeping changes, which significantly shaped his spiritual and intellectual pursuits. Lévi's early years were marked by the aftermath of the French Revolution, the Napoleonic Wars, and the restoration of the Bourbon monarchy. France was a society in transition, grappling with issues of national identity, the role of religion, and the impact of industrialization (Hobsbawn 1962). The lower classes were subjected to abject poverty, exacerbated by feudal remnants that limited their upward mobility. Meanwhile, the middle and upper classes found opportunities in emerging industries and commercial enterprises, deepening the socioeconomic divide (ibid.).

Lévi was born into a modest family, and his intellectual promise afforded him an ecclesiastical education. However, he found himself increasingly disillusioned with the Church, whose corruption and complicity in social inequality he could no longer ignore. It was a period of epistemological crisis for many; the Enlightenment ideals of reason and liberty had lost their luster amidst societal inequities, leading intellectuals to search for alternative frameworks for understanding and improving the human condition (ibid.). An ordained priest who eventually broke away from the Church, Lévi was drawn to socialist ideologies and profoundly influenced by the socialist currents of his time, particularly the works of Henri de Saint-Simon and Charles Fourier. Saint-Simon argued for a new social system in which the industrial class, the creators of social wealth, would replace the parasitic aristocracy. Fourier, on the other hand, envisioned a utopian society organized in "phalanxes" based on cooperative agriculture and small-scale industry.

Lévi's socialism was not merely an economic stance but a spiritually infused worldview. He saw socialism as a practical application of the fundamental Christian doctrine of human equality. For Lévi, the social question was essentially a religious one: How could society mirror the kingdom of God on Earth? His divergence from orthodoxy lay in his belief that achieving this would require not only spiritual but also social and economic transformations. These ideas were further developed in his works, most notably in *La Fable et le Dogme* and *Le Livre des Larmes*, where he expounded on the fusion of spirituality and social justice. However, Lévi's socialism would eventually shift as he became more deeply involved in occultism. While his initial socialist views were more aligned with a materialistic and egalitarian vision for society, his occult studies led him to a more hierarchical view. In the esoteric tradition, wisdom is a ladder, and Lévi began to see society in a similar way. Yet this did not mean a return to oppressive social structures; instead, he imagined a meritocracy of spiritual wisdom.

Herein lies the crux of Lévi's lifelong journey: an earnest attempt to reconcile material and spiritual aspirations, the worldly and the otherworldly. This was not just a personal quest but a microcosm of the greater socioeconomic and spiritual tensions of nineteenth-century France. Lévi was emblematic of a society grappling with new industrial powers, unprecedented scientific advancements, and ancient spiritual wisdom. His works, therefore, offer us a lens through which to explore these various ideas. His socialist leanings also informed his approach to magick and the occult, which he viewed as tools for personal and social transformation. Magick, for Lévi, was not about parlor tricks but about harnessing the unseen forces of the universe to bring about real-world change. In this way, he became a pivotal figure in the occult revival of the nineteenth century, infusing it with both the spiritual wisdom of ancient traditions and the pressing social concerns of his era. Through Lévi's intellectual and spiritual journey, one finds a nexus for much of his life's work, a point of fusion between his socialist commitments, his disillusionment with organized religion, and his deep dive into the mystical and the occult. It is at this very juncture that Baphomet takes its form—the form most recognizable today. This iconic representation, a complex symbol blending diverse elements of male, female, animal, and divine, encapsulates Lévi's lifetime quest to integrate the disparate forces at play in the universe, much like his quest to reconcile the socioeconomic divisions plaguing his contemporary society.

But why Baphomet? This bizarre figure, laden with such layered meaning, becomes in Lévi's hands the ultimate representation of the Great Work—the alchemical and spiritual objective of achieving the highest form of wisdom and enlightenment. Baphomet is not just an idol or a shallow emblem but rather a multidimensional key designed to unlock profound mysteries.

It is an occult icon that serves as a mirror reflecting the era's social discontent, spiritual yearning, and the perpetual human quest for understanding beyond mundane existence. Much like Baphomet, Lévi has become a prism through which the light of diverse intellectual currents of his time are refracted, illuminating a pathway that would be tread by esoteric scholars, social reformers, and spiritual seekers for generations to come. For Lévi, Baphomet becomes the quintessential symbol of an age teetering on the edge of reason and faith, materialism and spirituality, revolution and tradition. Baphomet is, in a way, his answer to the chaos: a visualization that both poses questions and offers solutions, that challenges boundaries while suggesting a harmonious synthesis.

With this in mind, let's take a deeper look at the man behind the icon and uncover just how Lévi's Baphomet becomes a transhistorical and transcultural symbol—not just a static image but a dynamic, living archetype continually resurrected in new forms from the drawing boards of Victorian occultists to the digital platforms of twenty-first-century mystics. The depths to which this symbol has penetrated modern esoteric thought cannot be overstated, and as we transition from the socioeconomic upheavals that framed Lévi's life to the chimeric, many-faced form of Baphomet, we are taking the next logical step in this fascinating journey. So, I invite you, fellow traveler, to keep your eyes and mind wide open as we venture into a world where symbols are not just artistic renderings but keys to cosmic riddles, where the quest for wisdom unfolds and the legacy of a nineteenth-century socialist Catholic priest–turned–mystic finds its most enduring artistic and spiritual expression.

Chapter 3

CRAFTING A SYMBOL
Éliphas Lévi, the Architect
of the Modern Baphomet

Everything lives by movement, everything is maintained
by equilibrium, and harmony results from the analogy of
contraries; this law is the form of forms.

—ÉLIPHAS LÉVI, *Transcendental Magic, Its Doctrine and Ritual*

In the sociopolitical chaos of mid-nineteenth century French intellectualism, few figures are as influential and complicated as Éliphas Lévi, certainly a man of his time yet timeless in his influence. He was not just an occultist but a revolutionary thinker whose magnum opus was an amalgamation of the base metals of politics, religion, and esotericism. Lévi emerged as a figure whose contributions to occultism, theology, and sociopolitical thought continue to be scrutinized by scholars and enthusiasts alike. At first glance, one might be tempted to pigeonhole him as a ceremonial magician or a purveyor of arcane symbolism. However, such a reductionist view would be a disservice to a man whose life and work were a living testament to the interconnectedness of all knowledge.

Lévi was born Alphonse Louis Constant in 1810 in Paris, and his humble beginnings were far removed from the status he would later attain (Strube 2017). The son of a struggling shoe-maker, Constant sought solace and intellectual stimulation at Saint-Sulpice seminary. However, the seminary years were a period of disillusionment, and it became increasingly clear that the confines of ecclesiastical life could not contain his burgeon-ing intellectual curiosities, as they often challenged the doctrine of the day. During this time, Constant was drawn to the uto-pian ideas of social reformers like Charles Fourier and Henri de Saint-Simon. These influences were instrumental in his grow-ing ideological rift with the Church, culminating in his involve-ment in socialist activities that led to his imprisonment in 1841 (ibid.). This incarceration, far from breaking his spirit, triggered a transformative intellectual odyssey. The subsequent years saw Constant, now under the pseudonym Éliphas Lévi (see Figure 8), dedicating himself to the mysteries of the arcane and distancing himself from both the politics that had imperiled him and the religious orthodoxy that had stifled him.

Lévi's pseudonym was not merely a superficial alias but sym-bolized a rupture from his past; a Hebraic reinterpretation of his birth name, it marked a new phase in his intellectual voyage (ibid.). While Lévi never explicitly detailed the reason-ing behind his choice of pen name in his writings, given the rich esoteric and religious traditions from which the name is derived, it is widely speculated that he chose it to reflect his deep engagement with Kabbalistic, Hermetic, and alchem-ical traditions. The name itself serves as a kind of mission statement, encapsulating his intent to synthesize various streams of religious and esoteric thought into a unified system.

Figure 8: Éliphas Lévi

While we can't be certain of his exact motivations for choosing this particular name, its resonance with the themes that pervade his work suggests that it was a carefully considered decision meant to encapsulate his life's work and philosophical pursuits. Éliphas, for example, is a Gallicized form of the Hebrew name אֱלִיפַז (Elifaz), which is a compound of two elements:

El, signifying "God," and *paz*, meaning "fine gold." Thus, the name can be interpreted to mean "God of Fine Gold" or "God is [my] Fine Gold." This part of his name resonates strongly with alchemical traditions, where the transformation of base metals into gold serves as both a physical and spiritual metaphor for the quest for wisdom and enlightenment. The term *fine gold* could be seen as an alchemical symbol for the ultimate goal of spiritual perfection. On the other hand, *Lévi* is derived from the Hebrew name לֵוִי (Levi), which means "to join" or "to accompany." In the biblical context, the Levites were the tribe designated for religious duties, serving as the spiritual "binders" or "joiners" of the community to God. When combined, the name Éliphas Lévi could imply a mission of spiritual alchemy: to synthesize various religious, esoteric, and philosophical traditions into a unified system under the divine wisdom symbolized by fine gold. In essence, the name serves as a declaration of Lévi's intent to act as a spiritual guide, aiding others in their quest for enlightenment by amalgamating diverse spiritual paths into a coherent and unified system. However, Lévi's engagement with occultism was not a retreat into obscurantism but rather a bold endeavor to synthesize disparate traditions, ranging from Kabbalah and Hermeticism to Rosicrucianism.

Lévi's seminal work, *Dogme et Rituel de la Haute Magie*, for instance, resonates as a cornerstone in occult literature (Strube 2017). What set this book apart was not just its exploration of the arcane but its accessibility and readability. Lévi deftly merged intricate occult themes with a clarity of prose, appealing beyond the realm of occultism and into the broader intellectual currents of his time. *Dogme et Rituel de la Haute Magie* captivated not only occult practitioners but also intellectual luminaries and artists.

W. B. Yeats, for instance, admired Lévi's capacity to wed mystical ideas with rational argumentation (Ellenberger 1970). Lévi's approach seemed to dovetail with the larger Romantic movement of the period, which sought a reenchantment of the world through the recovery or invention of myths, symbols, and rituals that could speak to the depths of human experience.

The text was more than a mere guide to ritualistic magick; it was an intellectually stimulating treatise that dared to bridge the chasm between the sacred and the profane. His work echoed post-Enlightenment philosophers like Voltaire who were skeptical of dogmatic beliefs, yet Lévi described Voltaire as having a "sneering and derisive philosophy" (Lévi 1861). It was as if Lévi had taken the profundity of ancient spiritual mysteries and distilled them through the lens of Enlightenment rationalism. This unique blend made the book an instant bestseller, expanding its influence beyond confined occult circles and into the intellectual salons that were the crucibles of nineteenth-century thought. The tome thus stands as an emblematic work, encapsulating the tensions and aspirations of an era wrestling with spiritual ennui and hungering for a synthesis of the mystical and the rational. This eclectic blend of influences and ideas lent the work a timeless quality, inspiring generations of occultists, artists, and thinkers alike, who found in its pages a pathway to transcending the limitations of conventional wisdom.

The Icon

While the mysterious figure of Baphomet traces its vague outlines back to the time of the Knights Templar, it was Lévi who brought form to this powerful but formless force, codifying its symbolic language and thereby laying the foundation for its future interpretations in the occult and beyond (Strube 2017). Lévi's image of the force that is Baphomet melded varied elements—a pentagram, a goat's head, an "as above, so below" posture—each steeped in historical and philosophical significance (see Figure 9). Lévi, the indefatigable polymath, seems to have embarked on an esoteric venture to amalgamate these multifarious symbolisms into a single icon. He looked at the Kabbalistic roots of the pentagram, an emblem of man and microcosm, while the goat's head was drawn from pagan and perhaps even pre-Abrahamic traditions. These symbols were not arbitrarily chosen; they were deliberate choices that aimed to condense myriad ideologies into a unified, intelligible form (ibid.). Lévi's portrayal of Baphomet as an amalgamation of male, female, and androgynous elements, along with the incorporation of various religious and esoteric symbols (such as the pentagram and the caduceus), offered a nuanced and multilayered representation of the figure. His Baphomet became more than just a mere idol; it was a symbolic lexicon that invited interpretation and contemplation. It became an *icon*.

This aspect of Lévi's Baphomet resonates strongly with the multiplicity and complexity of Kabbalistic thought and Hermetic philosophy, both of which seek to understand the underlying unity in apparent dualities (ibid.). Contrary to popular misconceptions that often associate it with Satanism or anti-Christian sentiments, Lévi's Baphomet is a nuanced representation of the equilibrium of opposites. It is deeply rooted in magnetistic theories and serves as a visual embodiment of Lévi's concept of the Astral Light. This alchemical fusion of disparate elements— politics, religion, and esotericism—into a harmonious whole reflects Lévi's broader intellectual project, which sought to

Figure 9: Baphomet as drawn in Éliphas Lévi, Dogme et Rituel de la Haute Magie *(Paris: Ancienne Librairie Germer-Baillière et Cie, 1855)*

synthesize these various streams of thought into a unified theory (ibid.). In many ways, he was a forerunner to modern esotericism's engagement with symbolism and comparative religion. He paved the way for figures like Arthur Edward Waite, an influential figure in Western esotericism, who was deeply impacted by Lévi's work.

Rider–Waite Tarot: The Devil Card

The evolution of the Devil card in tarot reveals a great deal about the shifting tides of esoteric and philosophical thought over time. Waite drew heavily upon Lévi's symbolic richness in designing the Rider–Waite Tarot deck, particularly the Devil card. In his design, Waite steered away from the simplicity of the Devil in the Tarot de Marseille deck, one of the most widely used tarot decks at that time (see Figure 10). The Tarot de Marseille, often referred to as the Marseilles Tarot, is a standard tarot pattern from which many other tarot decks derive. Originating in the seventeenth century in the city of Marseilles, France, this deck is primarily used for the purpose of divination, though it has also been used in games and various esoteric studies. The seventy-eight-card deck is rich in symbolism and draws from a variety of sources, including Christian mysticism, astrology, alchemy, and ancient mythology. The deck is known for its vivid colors and intricate designs, and it has been the subject of numerous interpretations and commentaries.

Before Lévi's influence, the Devil card in Waite's deck portrayed a fairly standard representation of the Christian devil— horns, bat wings, and an expression that is both menacing and mocking. This imagery is rooted in Judeo-Christian conceptions of evil, and the card often carried with it a straightforward moralizing message about temptation, bondage, and spiritual peril (Decker, Dummett, and Depaulis 1996). However, the Devil card underwent a profound transformation after the introduction of Lévi's work, particularly his conceptualization of Baphomet (see Figure 11). Where the Tarot de Marseille Devil is a symbol of straightforward malevolence, Lévi's Baphomet is a more

Figure 10: The original Devil card from a
Tarot de Marseille deck dating from 1701
CE to 1715 CE by Jean Dodal (Bibliotèque
Nationale de France)

nuanced figure, embodying dualities and serving as an amalgamation of various religious and philosophical ideas. Baphomet's
hermaphroditic form, for example, suggests a merging or balance of masculine and feminine energies, far removed from the
binary morality represented in earlier tarot decks. Additionally,
the chains that bind the humans in the card, the "as above, so
below" gesture, and the horned figure all can be traced back to
Lévi's illustration of Baphomet. It is as if Waite saw in Lévi's

work not just a symbol but a kind of mystical lexicon that could be incorporated into the tarot, which itself is a complex tableau of symbolism and interpretation (Huson 1980).

The linkage between Lévi's work and Waite's, especially in the realm of tarot, is an important touchstone in the history of Western esotericism. The Devil card serves as an homage of sorts to Lévi's Baphomet, albeit filtered through Waite's own Christian mysticism. Thus, through the lens of Lévi's Baphomet, the Devil card evolved from a one-dimensional moral warning to a multifaceted symbol inviting interpretation.

Figure 11: The Devil card from the Rider–Waite Tarot deck, ca. 1909

This transformation reflects broader changes in Western intellectual and spiritual landscapes, marking a shift from religious dogmatism toward a more integrative and interpretive approach to spirituality and morality. Lévi's Baphomet serves as a pivotal point in this transition, capturing the zeitgeist of an era rife with both religious questioning and spiritual exploration. The subsequent Rider–Waite Devil card, imbued with the complexity of Lévi's Baphomet, stands as a testament to this transformation, inviting us to engage with the arcane symbols and meanings that have accrued around this figure over time (Strube 2017; Hutton 2001). Like Lévi, Waite was concerned with the reconciliation of opposites and the potential for transcendence through symbolic understanding (Hutton 2001). The Rider–Waite Tarot deck, much like *Dogme et Rituel de la Haute Magie*, is laden with intricate symbolism designed to provoke deep introspection and contemplation, serving as a tool for spiritual evolution. Lévi's choice of elements for his Baphomet is no less than an academic study in semiotics. He seemed to delve deep into the philosophical underpinnings behind every line he drew and every symbol he incorporated. Was his Baphomet a hermetic attempt to reconcile cosmic dualities?

The male and the female, the celestial and the chthonic, the good and the evil: each found a place in Lévi's composite image. To understand his Baphomet is to unravel the complex lattice of his metaphysical assumptions—a lattice that beautifully blended mystical, Rosicrucian, Kabbalistic, and Hermetic traditions into an intricate and harmonious whole (Hanegraaff 1997). Further enhancing the narrative texture are the tensions between Lévi the occultist and Lévi the intellectual. He was deeply entrenched in the world of nineteenth-century academia yet found himself irresistibly drawn to the esoteric realms that traditional scholarly circles often derided. The attention to detail in his Baphomet figure, the references to Hermetic traditions, the nods to Kabbalistic symbolism—all reveal a man who couldn't settle for either a purely academic or purely mystical viewpoint. Instead, he chose a groundbreaking path, a third way, that sought to integrate the mystical into the intellectual and vice versa (Strube 2017). Perhaps this is one of the most understated yet poignant characteristics of Lévi's work: the art of synthesis. He was reading, integrating, and even challenging the works of Enlightenment philosophers and thinkers while crafting an emblem that itself is a syncretic piece of art, a fusion of the rational and the mystical (Lévi 1861).

The Sigils

A *sigil* is a symbol or emblem with roots in the Latin word *sigillum*, which translates to "seal." The word *sigil* is pronounced as /ˈsɪdʒ.ɪl/, with the stress on the first syllable. In various esoteric and mystical traditions, a sigil serves as a visual representation of a specific intention, concept, or spiritual entity. Historically, these symbols have been employed in grimoires (ancient manuals of magick) to encapsulate complex spiritual processes or beings in a singular, easily reproducible form. The primary function of a sigil is to act as a focal point for the practitioner's will and intent, often serving as a conduit for invoking spiritual forces or manifesting specific outcomes.

The Sigil of Baphomet, as we understand it today, often diverges from Lévi's original sketch, yet they share a common lineage that can be traced back to various esoteric traditions.

This symbol, usually a goat's head encased within an inverted pentagram (a five-pointed star), has become almost synonymous with modern conceptions of Baphomet and is often associated with occultism, especially modern branches of Satanism and contemporary occult groups. The Sigil itself is not directly Lévi's creation; it has a far older and more complex origin. Its components, however, are deeply connected to his esoteric formulations. The downward-facing point traditionally symbolizes matter taking precedence over the spirit, aligning with the Sigil's oft-attributed anti-establishment undertones. The pentagram has been employed in various cultures for thousands of years—from the ancient Greeks, who associated it with the goddess Hygieia (representative of health), to the Pythagoreans, who saw in it mathematical perfection. It has been associated with the *golden ratio*, a mathematical ratio often found in nature and considered aesthetically pleasing in art and architecture. It can be drawn using a continuous line, representing unity and wholeness, but its inversion, as found in the Sigil of Baphomet, has been interpreted as a reversal or subversion of these traditional virtues.

Lévi introduced the concept of the pentagram as a potent magickal sign, representing a myriad of dualities: intellectual omnipotence or confusion, divine or diabolical attributes, victory or defeat, and more. This symbol, with its star of five points, has roots in ancient traditions, including Gnostic schools where it was called the Blazing Star. Lévi further elaborated that the orientation of the pentagram's points could symbolize various attributes, divine or diabolic. Lévi's pentagram served as a graphic codification of alchemical, Kabbalistic, and mythological motifs. It was a cosmic diagram signifying not just the universe but also the moral, intellectual, and spiritual states of humankind.

Fast-forward to 1897, and we find another key moment in the evolution of the Sigil of Baphomet in the works of French poet and occultist Stanislas de Guaita. His book, *La Clef de la Magie Noire (The Key to Black Magic)*—a significant work in the realm of esoteric studies that delved into various aspects of magickal practices and symbolism—incorporated two distinct sigils: an upright pentacle (circled pentagram) depicting the face of Adam, and an inverted pentacle with a goat's face, clearly influenced by Lévi's original concept (see Figure 12).

Figure 12: Sigils depicted in Stanislas de Guaita, La Clef de la Magie Noire [The Key to Black Magic] *(Paris: Chamuel, 1897). The upright and inverted pentagrams represent spirit over matter (holiness) and matter over spirit (evil), respectively.*

De Guaita, a Rosicrucian and a considerable figure in French occult circles, used this symbolism to explore ideas related to duality and spiritual tension, specifically the concepts of "spirit over matter" (holiness) and its opposite, "matter over spirit" (evil). In his upright sigil, the four lower points of the pentagram symbolize the four classical elements—earth, water, air, and fire—that make up the material world. The uppermost point of the pentagram represents the spirit, signifying its dominion over matter. This arrangement encapsulates the dualistic nature of existence, contrasting the spiritual and the material, and serves as a complex symbol used for various esoteric and magickal purposes. This pentacle also incorporates the Hebrew letter shin (ש) into the *tetragrammaton*—the four-letter divine name Yod-He-Vav-He (יהוה)—to produce the *pentagrammaton*: an esoteric variation of the Hebrew name for Jesus (ישוע), Yeshua (יהשוה). Thus, this sigil is associated with positive Judeo-Christian spiritual principles.

In contrast, De Guaita's inverted sigil with the goat's head is often associated with darker or occult forces. It includes references to Samael and Lilith (both figures commonly found in Jewish mysticism and Kabbalistic tradition) and incorporates the Hebrew name for Leviathan, which often symbolizes chaos and the abyss.

Although Lévi's original Baphomet sketch and de Guaita's sigils share thematic elements related to dualism, elemental forces, and spiritual dominion over the material, they are distinct in their historical development, specific associations, and orientation. While de Guaita's inverted sigil includes Kabbalistic and infernal elements, Lévi's original Baphomet sketch is a more general synthesis of various esoteric and mythological themes.

Lévi's illustration does not include the specific Judeo-Christian elements found in de Guaita's pentacles.

As it is commonly recognized today, the Sigil of Baphomet borrows heavily from de Guaita's inverted sigil: it features a goat's head within an inverted pentagram and is likewise associated with occult and potentially dark qualities. Its first documented use is generally attributed to the Church of Satan, founded by Anton LaVey in 1966. LaVey adopted the symbol as an emblem for his new religious movement, solidifying its association with modern Satanism (LaVey 1969). While it also owes much to Lévi's interpretation of Baphomet, LaVey's Sigil of Baphomet differs considerably in context and meaning.

The Sigil has evolved from its early Gnostic and Pythagorean roots to encapsulate various theological, esoteric, and philosophical doctrines. Over time, it has come to serve as a robust emblem, replete with meanings that span cultures and historical periods but always symbolizing a powerful array of dualities and magickal potentials. When we consider the Pythagorean roots of the pentagram alongside the representation of the Egyptian Neter Amon ("hidden one") as the Goat of Mendes, we can discern a syncretism by which the Sigil becomes not merely a sign but a multidimensional representation of cosmological and metaphysical ideologies, uniting elements from Egyptian, Hebrew, and Greco-Roman contexts.

In contemporary times, the Sigil of Baphomet has been appropriated for various uses, from shock-rock album covers to iconography for various esoteric orders. As a result, it has been subject to numerous copyright claims, most notably from the Church of Satan, which has led to some restrictions on its use. Yet it remains a compelling symbol that, despite its relative youth, has roots that dig deep into the soil of esoteric tradition. Thus, the Sigil of Baphomet serves as both an innovation and an amalgamation. It is a composite of earlier esoteric symbols reinterpreted through modern lenses. It captures the zeitgeist of the era in which it was popularized, while still echoing the complex history and multifaceted symbolism that preceded it. Like Lévi's original conception of Baphomet, it is a chimeric symbol—part goat, part star, and wholly representative of the multifaceted nature of occult practices and beliefs.

Figures like Lévi stood at this unique crossroads, attempting to reconcile the past with the present, the East with the West, and the sacred with the secular (Owen 2004). Lévi's enduring legacy lies in his ability to take these disparate themes and craft them into a coherent, albeit intricate, metaphysical worldview. His Baphomet served as a keystone in this edifice, a symbol that encapsulated the vast array of philosophies and traditions he sought to unify. To this end, Baphomet transcended its origins to become an archetype, a potent cultural signifier that has been adapted, appropriated, and reinterpreted across time and space. Whether encountered in the mysterious pages of a nineteenth-century grimoire or recognized in a modern adaptation like the Sigil of Baphomet, it invites us to ponder the complexity of spiritual symbolism and its continual evolution. Baphomet serves as an enduring testament to human ingenuity and the inexorable drive to make sense of the unfathomable facets of existence (Strube 2017).

As part of Lévi's occult opus, Baphomet was imbued with significance that transcended the literal interpretation of demonic idolatry. Lévi conceived Baphomet as a symbol of the "perennial philosophy," a term borrowed from Gottfried Wilhelm Leibniz but popularized by the likes of Aldous Huxley in the twentieth century. This philosophy posits a universal truth at the heart of all spiritual traditions—a convergence of religion, science, and metaphysics. In his quest to illustrate this grand unification of wisdom, Lévi rendered a potent symbol that still reverberates across esoteric studies (ibid.). His synthesis of religious and esoteric symbols from diverse traditions echoed the eclecticism that would become a hallmark of the New Age movement, albeit in a more disciplined and scholarly form (Hanegraaff 1997).

Lighting the Path

According to Strube (2017), the Astral Light (*lumière astrale*) is a foundational element in Lévi's iconic drawing of Baphomet. Specifically, Baphomet is described as an embodiment of the Astral Light, a concept central to—and perhaps the best-known aspect of—Lévi's magickal theory.

Contrary to occultist perspectives and to recent scholarship, Lévi did not rely on ancient, medieval, or even early modern sources when he developed this theory. He pointed out himself that he had borrowed the concept of the Astral Light from "the school of Pasqualis Martinez" (i.e., Martinism). However, his actual sources came not from the late eighteenth century but from the 1850s. Most likely, he discovered the notion in a publication from 1852, "La magie devoilée" by Jean Du Potet de Sennevoy, which Lévi explicitly named as a source. He agreed with Du Potet's conviction that the Astral Light denoted an *agent magique* that had been known to the Kabbalists, the Chaldean mages, the alchemists, and the Gnostics. As a formative medium (*médiateur plastique*), it was the force behind magnetism and consequently the ultimate cause of magickal operations (ibid., p. 30). Lévi described the Astral Light as a "blind mechanism" that worked "mathematically" and followed immutable laws (ibid., p. 30). However, the will (*volonté*) of the magician was needed to control it. Lévi took great pains to distinguish this theory from other magnetistic approaches, especially from somnambulism—hence his ongoing polemics against "dabblers." In his view, the true practitioner of magick needed two fundamental qualifications: first, a natural disposition and individual training of the "will," and second, an "initiation" (ibid., p. 30).

Lévi's Baphomet serves as a visual codification of this Astral Light, amalgamating various symbols and elements that are steeped in historical and philosophical significance (ibid.). In essence, Lévi's Baphomet is not just a mere symbol but a complex representation that encapsulates the Astral Light's multifaceted nature. It is a visual lexicon that aims to express the equilibrium of cosmic dualities—male and female, celestial and chthonic, good and evil—each finding a place in this composite image. The Astral Light, therefore, is not just an abstract concept but is made manifest in the very form and symbolism of Baphomet, serving as a focal point for understanding the intricate lattice of Lévi's metaphysical assumptions (ibid.) Thus, to comprehend Lévi's Baphomet is to delve into his understanding of the Astral Light, an understanding he meticulously developed in the context of nineteenth-century spiritualistic magnetism and through his critiques against contemporary Catholic writers. The Astral Light is the underpinning force that brings coherence to the diverse elements present in the figure of Baphomet.

Through his meticulous synthesis of tarot symbolism, alchemical wisdom, and Kabbalistic insights, Lévi articulated a living symbol that resists easy categorization. The goatee-bearded, androgynous Baphomet with the caduceus, as birthed from Lévi's pen, became the yardstick against which future generations would measure their understanding of this sometimes infamous figure. While Baphomet may have accrued additional layers of interpretation and embroilment in various cultural battles, its core elements remain loyal to Lévi's vision. It serves as an indelible testament to Lévi's skill in synthesizing disparate strands of occult knowledge into a cohesive and striking image. Thus, Baphomet transforms under Lévi's care from an obscure medieval concoction into a multifaceted symbol, drawing from as far back as Egyptian lore and from fields as diverse as Gnosticism and ceremonial magick. As Lévi has shown us, the symbols we entertain—whether in our minds, etched in ancient manuscripts, or imprinted on modern paraphernalia—aren't merely static representations but dynamic entities, shaping and being shaped by the currents of thought they encounter. In this sense, Baphomet is as much a work of art as it is a spiritual riddle, ever-evolving yet grounded in a rich history that refuses to be forgotten. Lévi's Baphomet is both an archetype of hidden wisdom and a litmus test for our openness to explore the shadowy realms of the unknown.

As we close this chapter on Lévi's revolutionary rendition of Baphomet, let us turn our gaze to yet another alluring path on the quest for hidden knowledge: the secretive halls of Freemasonry and other secret societies. Lévi had a complex relationship with Freemasonry (ibid.). His magickal theory and concept of the Astral Light was developed in a context that was clearly inspired by Freemasonry; however, his engagement with the movement was more of a critique than an endorsement. Initially, he was highly skeptical of it. He saw Freemasonry as a gathering point for opposition during the 1850s, but he became a Freemason for only a short period before distancing himself from it and denouncing it sharply. Lévi's focus was on a superior "science" that would lead to the final synthesis of science, religion, and philosophy, a vision he felt Freemasonry failed to grasp (Strube 2017, p. 39); in short, he viewed the Freemasons as false representatives of a tradition they failed to understand. His skepticism was rooted in his belief that the Freemasons had lost the key to understanding the true tradition, a key he claimed to have rediscovered (ibid.). He wrote, "The Masonic associations of the present time are no less ignorant of the high meaning of their symbols than are the rabbins of the Sepher Yetzirah and the Zohar concerning the ascending scale of the three degrees, with the transverse progression from right to left and from left to right of the kabalistic septenary" (Lévi 1855/1896).

So while Freemasonry influenced Lévi's conceptual framework, especially his notion of initiation, he ultimately rejected the movement. This complex relationship reflects Lévi's broader project of synthesizing various religious, scientific, and philosophical traditions into a coherent magickal theory. What connections might we find between the concealed rites of the Freemasons and the iconic figure of Baphomet? Could it be that these guarded brotherhoods hold keys to unlocking further layers of this symbol's meaning? As we will discover, the veiled world of Masonic lodges and ritualistic orders offers an expansive new theatre wherein Baphomet has played roles in the service of both the Great Work and those seeking to snuff out the Light.

Chapter 4

TRACING THE THREADS
Baphomet's Link to Freemasonry
and Secret Societies

*The Occult Science of the Ancient Magi was concealed
under the shadows of the Ancient Mysteries[,] it
was imperfectly revealed or rather disfigured by the
Gnostics: it is guessed at under the obscurities that cover
the pretended crimes of the Templars; and it is found
enveloped in enigmas that seem impenetrable, in the
Rights of the Highest Masonry.*

—ALBERT PIKE, *Morals and Dogma of the Ancient and
Accepted Scottish Rite of Freemasonry*

The eighteenth century marked a period of fervent intellectual exploration and can be considered the birthplace of
neo-Templarism (Bullock 1998). During this era, a wealth of
literature surfaced connecting the Freemasons with the historical Templars. Éliphas Lévi was deeply influenced by these
writings, notably by the work of Austrian orientalist Joseph
von Hammer-Purgstall in 1818. Hammer-Purgstall contended
that the Templars were involved in Gnostic practices and

worshipped Baphomet, a claim that resonated within the fertile intellectual climate of France (Hammer-Purgstall 1818/2017). His theories reinvigorated discussions about long-standing accusations against the Templars and further linked them to the Kabbalistic tradition. As the century progressed, these neo-Templar threads became intricately woven into Freemasonry (Mackey 1873). The Masonic Templar legend claimed that persecuted Templars took refuge in Scotland, a narrative that gained prominence after a key document was published in Strasbourg in 1760 (Coil 1996). Although this legend fueled the development of various Masonic systems, it was not universally accepted. Friedrich Nicolai, a German publisher, questioned the historicity of the Templar legend and its confluence with Freemasonry (Nicolai 1781/1782).

Conversely, Augustin Barruel (1797) constructed an elaborate conspiracy theory that attributed the ideological underpinnings of the French Revolution to Kabbalistic Freemasons, Templars, and Gnostics, among others. In France, this evolving narrative fueled debates during the 1770s and contributed to the establishment of prominent Masonic organizations (Dyer 2003). By the early nineteenth century, this complex narrative had inspired a wave of Masonic literature that painted Freemasonry in a favorable light. Although Lévi didn't explicitly mention these works, evidence suggests he was familiar with them (Lévi 1855/1896). For instance, when reviewing J.M. Ragon's *Orthodoxie maçonnique*, Lévi lauded its attempt to imbue Freemasonry with a coherent "occult philosophy," despite his reservations about the book's anti-Christian stance (Lévi 1855/1896; Ragon 1853). Lévi's own characterization of Baphomet seemed to reflect influences from this earlier Masonic and anti-Masonic literature, revealing the layered complexities that had evolved since the second half of the eighteenth century (Lévi 1855/1896).

Common Threads

As we advance in our understanding of Western esoteric thought, the Kabbalah emerges as a single connecting thread that weaves through various mystical traditions, holding them together in a mysterious dance of symbolism and wisdom (see Figure 13). Take, for instance, Baphomet and the layers of symbolism that find parallel in the Kabbalistic Tree of Life. The Tree, representing both the divine structure of the universe and the human soul, becomes an archetypal blueprint mirrored in the complex symbols of Masonic rites and the perplexing image of Baphomet, a

Figure 13: The emblem of the nineteenth-century Ordre kabbalistique de la Rose-Croix *society, founded in 1888 in Paris by Joséphin Péladan and Stanislas de Guaita*

deity teeming with manifold meanings (Scholem 1941; Hall 1928). While mainstream Freemasonry doesn't explicitly affiliate with any particular magickal or mystical system, gravitating as much toward rationalism as mysticism, there are subsets of Masons, as there are with the Rosicrucians. These groups may choose to apply magickal or "hermetic" interpretations to Masonic rituals, exercising their right within the fraternity's nondogmatic approach.

Often considered inheritors of some Templar mysteries, the Rosicrucians seamlessly incorporated elements from various mystical traditions into their philosophies, including the Kabbalah. It is speculated that their syncretic approach could be a continuation of Templar secrets, ones that might even involve the figure of Baphomet (McIntosh 1998). Adding to the complexity, consider for a moment that the legendary Knights Templar, who many argue had strong Gnostic and perhaps Kabbalistic inclinations, may have been influenced by Sufi mysticism. The Sufis' quest for direct experience with the divine—expressed through elaborate rituals and symbolism—resonates with the Kabbalistic Tree of Life and the Masonic ascent toward enlightenment (Trimingham 1998). Another secret society, the Martinist Order, does not directly mention Baphomet yet is deeply committed to exploring dualities and the reconciliation thereof, an idea that is quintessentially Kabbalistic in nature (Waite 1901). Theosophists, again, while not explicitly tied to the Templars or Baphomet, also dance on the edges of duality and mystical symbolism. Founded by Helena Petrovna Blavatsky, this society navigated through Eastern philosophies but still found the Kabbalah relevant enough to integrate into its esoteric framework (Blavatsky 1888).

Through this panoramic lens, the Kabbalah is revealed not merely as an esoteric curiosity but as a foundational pillar in an intricate network of mystical traditions. From the Rosicrucians' alchemical pursuits to the Theosophical Society's cosmic quests, from the symbols adorning Masonic lodges to the equally mysterious deity known as Baphomet, the imprints of Kabbalah are unmistakable. This journey through Western esoteric thought paints a picture not just of isolated groups and ideas, but of an expansive landscape where wisdom flows like a subterranean river, emerging here and there to nourish diverse mystical traditions. It offers us an opportunity to witness the magnificent scope and interconnectedness of esoteric wisdom, revealing how even the most disparate traditions can converge at the wellspring of Kabbalistic thought. However, a word of caution is in order. The threads connecting these diverse traditions often appear more as faint echoes rather than clear, definitive lines (Hanegraaff 1997). The temptation to draw straightforward conclusions is indeed strong, but the evidence reminds us to approach these intersections with a keen sense of scholarly discernment. Nevertheless, the presence of Kabbalistic interpretations within Freemasonry has led certain Christian factions to label Freemasonry as "satanic." This claim is frequently leveled against any secret society that possesses ritualistic practices for its initiates.

Baphomet Worship

Numerous Masonic denouncers utilize quotes from Albert Pike's *Morals and Dogma* to attempt to "demonstrate" that Masons revere Lucifer, who is often consumed. The frequently cited section (Chapter XIX, p. 321) states:

> *The Apocalypse is, to those who receive the nineteenth*
> *Degree, the Apotheosis of that Sublime Faith which*

> *aspires to God alone, and despises all the pomps and*
> *works of Lucifer. LUCIFER, the Light-bearer! Strange*
> *and mysterious name to give to the Spirit of Darkness!*
> *Lucifer, the Son of the Morning! Is it he who bears the*
> *Light, and with its splendors intolerable blinds feeble,*
> *sensual, or selfish Souls? Doubt it not! for traditions are*
> *full of Divine Revelations and Inspirations: and Inspira-*
> *tion is not of one Age nor of one Creed. Plato and Philo,*
> *also, were inspired. (Pike 1871)*

Certain Masons rebut the critics who leverage this passage as proof of Freemasonry's satanic inclinations, arguing that these critics overlook the passage's initial part while focusing on Lucifer's association with Light. They alternatively reason that if a) Pike deems the works of Plato and Philo to be as divinely inspired as the Apocalypse of Saint John, and b) Plato and Philo were pre-Christian pagans, and c) all pagan beliefs are satanic, then it implies that d) Pike (and by extension, Freemasonry) indulges in Satan worship. However, other Masons refute this simply by emphasizing that Masonry is nondogmatic. Therefore, Pike's views are his personal interpretations, which may now be considered somewhat outdated. Although the Roman Catholic Church has condemned Freemasonry repeatedly, it does not explicitly label it as satanic.

It was not uncommon to include references to Baphomet in such hoaxes. In 1896, Arthur Edward Waite—notable occultist, unconventional scholar, and co-designer of the well-known Rider-Waite Tarot deck—unveiled his work *Devil-worship in France; or, The Question of Lucifer; a Record of Things Seen and Heard in the Secret Societies According to the Evidence of Initiates.* The book explores the initiation ritual of the Palladian Rite of Freemasonry,

the apex of the Masonic rites hierarchy, orchestrated by Albert
Pike. Pike proposed the idea of a dual divinity, where Lucifer
equals God in power (Pike 1871) and was worshipped in this particular Freemason rite (ibid.). The term *Palladian* in the Palladian
Rite is derived from *Pallas*, referencing the Greek entity Pallas—
the progeny of the original werewolf Lycaon, and the mentor of
Athena, the goddess of wisdom and warfare.

In 1880, aboard the steamboat *Anadyr*, Dr. Bataille encountered a dying Italian silk merchant named Gaëtano Carbuccia,
who revealed to him the demonic ceremonies of the Palladian Rite of Freemasonry. Intrigued, Dr. Bataille embarked on
a worldwide journey to infiltrate these rituals, publishing his
findings roughly a decade later. His exploration led him to witness what took place behind the secret doors of the Palladian
lodges. One account described a ritual where initiates revered
an altar dedicated to Baphomet, adorned with the skulls of three
Masonic martyrs, one of them Jacques de Molay. As per the
narrative, Lucifer manifested in a radiant physical form while
they worshipped. A similar ritual in Sri Lanka involved a seemingly lifeless woman suddenly crawling to an altar beneath a
Baphomet statue and being burned alive by lodge members as
they chanted demonic incantations.

Dr. Bataille's investigation led him to a French colonial out-
post in India, where he was confronted with a ghastly sight.
The barely ventilated area was filled with a disgusting smell of
decay (Waite 1896/2016). Lodge members had been congregating
around a Baphomet statue for so long that they were deterio-
rating, their bodies ravaged by infected skin ulcers. Rats gnawed
on the faces of some worshippers, barely sentient quasi corpses
reeking of gangrene. One particularly horrifying sight was an

initiate's eyeball hanging out of its socket and swinging beside the man's cheek. Whenever he attempted to utter the name Beelzebub, his loose eyeball would roll into his mouth, muffling his speech (ibid.) When attempts to summon a demon by these invocations failed, a woman was burned at the altar. When that didn't succeed, a white goat was brought forth. The grand master placed the goat on the Baphomet altar, tortured it, set it ablaze, and gutted it so that its innards could be strewn on the steps, all while the participants committed horrifying blasphemies against God. Their final attempt was to slit the throat of a half-dead worshipper. Despite all these efforts, no demon manifested. Dr. Bataille persisted with his ethnographical study of Palladium Freemasons, recording numerous instances of animal sacrifices, human levitation, and necrophilia. He once reported seeing the demon Asmodeus materialize in a lodge and choose a human woman as his consort.

During a conference of the Geographic Society in Paris on April 19, 1897, however, a man named Marie Joseph Gabriel Antoine Jogand-Pagès stepped forward and declared that he was the originator of Dr. Bataille's testimonies. Jogand-Pagès, who wrote under the pseudonym Léo Taxil, asserted that it had all been an elaborate hoax designed to ridicule the Christian perspective of Freemasonry.

Taxil's hoax publications in the late nineteenth century played a critical role in the vilification of Freemasons. His works falsely claimed that Freemasonry was directly involved in Satan worship and ritualistic abuse, attributing much of this malevolence to Baphomet (see Figure 14). His writings weren't merely a concoction of imaginative fiction; they served a more insidious purpose (Waite 1896/2016). They aimed to vilify not just

Freemasonry, but all secret societies that held wisdom traditions alternative to the Christian orthodoxy of the time. This smear campaign was not a solitary instance but part of a larger narrative that drew upon older templates of religious rivalry, heresy, and the fear of the "other."

Figure 14: Baphomet at a Freemason session. Drawing by Pierre Méjanel and engraving by François Pannemaker. Source: Léo Taxil, Les Mystères de la Franc-Maçonnerie *(Paris, 1886).*

Even though Taxil's claims were eventually revealed as fraudulent, the damage was already done. The shadow he cast over Baphomet and, by extension, Freemasonry, continues to linger in the collective consciousness. Within this spectacle of vilification, the essence of the figure—the synthesis of duality, the reconciliation of opposites, and the spiritual ascent outlined in Kabbalistic wisdom—was lost. It is noteworthy that, historically, Kabbalistic thought has always embraced complexity, especially concerning the Divine. However, the demonization narrative reduced it to a mere prop in a theater of heresy and deceit (Howard 1989).

Another intriguing and convoluted case, the Morgan Affair, exposes the volatile mixture of secrecy, public perception, and journalistic overreach of the nineteenth century. In 1826, New York bricklayer William Morgan announced his intention to write a tell-all book unveiling the secret rituals of the Freemasons. His motives remain a subject of speculation—some say his plan was out of revenge for perceived slights within the order, while others argue it was a purely opportunistic attempt to make money. Whatever the reasons, Morgan set into motion a series of events that would have far-reaching consequences. Before his planned book could see the light of day, Morgan was arrested on questionable charges. Some allege these charges were fabricated to keep him silent. Not long afterward, he vanished without a trace. Rumors swirled about his fate; some said he was kidnapped and murdered to keep the secrets of Freemasonry safe, while others believed he had been paid to disappear. The fact remained: Morgan was gone, and in his wake, a storm of controversy erupted.

Morgan's disappearance wasn't just a criminal inquiry; it metamorphosed into a social and political lightning rod. The lack of a body, the murky circumstances of his disappearance, and the secret society implicated in his alleged murder created a fertile ground for rumor-mongering and mass hysteria. Newspapers, seizing the opportunity for a tantalizing story, fanned the flames of public anxiety. Articles speculated on the nefarious influence of the Masons, suggesting they had the power not only to make a man disappear but also to subvert justice and escape punishment. The public response was swift and severe. The first-ever third party in the United States, the Anti-Masonic Party, was born, representing a collective expression of the mistrust and resentment brewing against the Masonic order. Even reputable figures like future president Millard Fillmore and future secretary of state William H. Seward got swept up in the anti-Masonic sentiments. Ordinary Masons found themselves shunned by society, their loyalties questioned, and their activities monitored. Lodges lost members, and some even closed their doors, unable to withstand the onslaught of public scrutiny (Knight 1932).

While Freemasonry would recover in time, the Morgan Affair cast a long shadow over the institution, raising questions that still resonate. The saga highlighted the susceptibility of secret societies to public suspicion and demonstrated how easily such groups could become scapegoats for societal anxieties. Moreover, it exposed the power of the media in shaping public opinion, a lesson as relevant today as it was in the nineteenth century. The Morgan Affair serves as a cautionary tale about the fragile equilibrium between secretive organizations and the society that hosts them. It exemplifies how misunderstandings and concerns about hidden systems of knowledge can lead not only to stigmatization but also to tangible social and political ramifications. Far more than a simple crime story, the episode opens up a complex array of issues related to the influence of secret societies, the impact of public perception, and the potency of fear of the unknown.

This overt demonization had another unfortunate consequence: the obfuscation of the nuanced and esoteric roots of Baphomet, many of which are traceable to Kabbalistic thought. The Kabbalah itself is a repository of mystical Jewish wisdom, built upon an elaborate system of ten *sefirot* (divine emanations) representing an unfathomable God's multiple facets. As Moshe Idel (1988) argues in *Kabbalah: New Perspectives*, the intricate symbolism of the Kabbalah provides a window into understanding divine complexity. Within this framework, Baphomet can be seen as an amalgamation of these complexities—a figure that encompasses both the light and the dark, the male and the female, the spiritual and the material. However, when the spotlight turns to demonization, as Arthur Edward Waite suggests, the richness of these esoteric traditions often gets lost, distilled into simplified caricatures that serve partisan agendas (Waite 1896/2016).

One could argue that the very act of demonization is a corruption of Kabbalistic principles. In Kabbalah, even the darker sefirot are not evil in the Christian sense; they are necessary counterbalances in the cosmic equation. Demonizing Baphomet or any other figure with roots in this tradition is akin to taking a multifaceted diamond and judging it based on a single flaw while ignoring its overall brilliance. This corrupting tendency has real-world implications. In an era when secret societies are both vilified and romanticized, the complexity and nuance of their intellectual and spiritual traditions are often overshadowed by the sensational tales that Taxil and his ilk perpetuated.

The demonization of Baphomet served as an instrument to malign Freemasonry and other societies that bore esoteric wisdom (see Figure 15). This attack often eclipsed the richness of the traditions from which these groups drew, including the Kabbalistic frameworks that offer a balanced and complex understanding of divinity and existence. As we continue to dissect the

Figure 15: La femme et l'enfant dans la Franc-maconnerie universelle, *an anti-Masonic illustration featuring Baphomet by Abel Clarin de la Rive, ca. 1894*

nuances of Western esoteric thought, it is essential to recognize these figures and traditions for what they are—a complex interplay of ideas and symbols, far removed from the simplistic "good versus evil" narratives that have often been imposed upon them. In doing so, we can begin to unravel the misinterpretations and manipulations that have plagued these esoteric traditions for centuries, providing a clearer, more nuanced view that allows for both the light and shadow aspects of these complex systems. In that clarity, we find the opportunity for a more profound understanding of both self and cosmos.

The grand stage of Western esoteric thought is far from monolithic. Instead, it is a dynamic forum where diverse traditions and philosophies come to the fore, each contributing unique textures to the larger design. Whether it is the mystic allure of Kabbalistic wisdom deeply ingrained in Masonic rites or the fascinating (albeit often misunderstood) figure of Baphomet that has become a symbol of vilification, there's an undeniable richness that compels us to probe further. Perhaps the most intriguing and often disconcerting part of this exploration is the ease with which esoteric wisdom can be weaponized to engender fear, shape political landscapes, and rewrite cultural narratives. The Morgan Affair serves as an arresting testament to the power of misinformation fueled by the pervasive, latent anxieties around secrecy and hidden knowledge (Knight 1932). Just as William Morgan's disappearance gave rise to the Anti-Masonic Party, the demonization of countless esoteric symbols and teachings has trivialized profound philosophies that invite us to transcend our mundane understanding of the world.

The narrative that emerges is thus a double-edged sword. On one side, you have a sophisticated legacy of symbols, rituals, and philosophies that stretch back to ancient civilizations, probing the nature of reality and the human psyche. On the other, you have a reactionary culture that can, in its moments of weakness, cast aside nuance and contemplative understanding in favor of vilification and stigmatization (Hanegraaff 1997). However, this is where our journey gains its true purpose. Those on the Path are called to navigate the dark corridors of esoteric thought, not just to engage with the shadowy and the mysterious but rather to bring to light the dimensions of human understanding that remain elusive. How else would we be able to reconcile the duality between the spiritual and the mundane, as the Martinist order proposes (Waite 1901), or appreciate the Sufi wisdom that may have influenced the Knights Templar (Trimingham 1998)?

In preceding chapters, we've navigated spotty history and mythology that have enveloped Baphomet—a figure often subject to vilification and sensationalism. Yet much of this vilification emanates from the shrouded practices and encoded symbols of secret societies, leaving us with gaps in understanding that are too easily filled with prejudice or fear. The taboo that surrounds secret societies often magnifies these gaps, fueling societal unease and leaving room for unfounded claims to proliferate. However, as we venture into Chapter 5, it's important to distinguish between misunderstandings born out of secrecy and those provocative figures who intentionally wade into the darkness, amplifying the sinister lore that surrounds Baphomet. Among these figures, none stands out more prominently than Aleister Crowley, who relished his public image as "the wickedest man in the world." Unlike his misunderstood predecessors in esoteric traditions, Crowley reveled in the more ominous interpretations of Baphomet.

In the reawakening of occult interests that characterized the nineteenth and early twentieth centuries, Crowley took these esoteric symbols and intentionally draped them in layers of shadow and even malevolence. It was as if he took the whispered accusations against Baphomet—ones largely rooted in misconceptions—and gave them a form and a voice. For Crowley, Baphomet was no misunderstood symbol but instead a potent force, boldly linked to Satan himself. How did Crowley embrace and expand upon the dark allure often attributed to Baphomet? What practices and rituals did he employ in service of Baphomet, and to what extent did he shape the modern conception of Baphomet as a symbol of forbidden wisdom and darker forces?

Chapter 5

THE INTERSECTION OF THELEMA AND BAPHOMET
Aleister Crowley's Great Beast

The soul is beyond male and female as
it is beyond Life and Death.

—ALEISTER CROWLEY, *The Book of Lies*

The symbol of Baphomet has undergone various transformations throughout its long and storied history. While Éliphas Lévi
may have drawn what is perhaps the most famous depiction,
Aleister Crowley had his own unique interpretation. Crowley's
engagement with the concept of Baphomet is far from casual; it
is deeply embedded within his complex religious and magickal
system known as Thelema. Crowley was not content with mere
replication of historical symbols; instead, he sought to redefine,
reinterpret, and recontextualize them. His Baphomet diverges
significantly from prior renderings, notably those of Lévi, transforming it into a complex theological construct that engages
directly with Thelemic doctrines. Crowley's interpretation of
Baphomet emerges as an idiosyncratic strand within the larger,
complicated web of Baphomet's history and significance. This

reconstruction of Baphomet serves as a lens through which one can view the broader contours of Crowley's metaphysical landscape.

The Great Beast

Aleister Crowley (see Figure 16) was born Edward Alexander Crowley on October 12, 1875, in Royal Leamington Spa, England, into a wealthy and devoutly religious family associated with a conservative Christian sect known as the Plymouth Brethren (Sutin 2002). Despite this upbringing—or perhaps in defiance of it—Crowley would go on to become a groundbreaking and controversial occultist, ceremonial magician, and writer. Crowley was as complex as he was controversial. He was a prolific writer, with works ranging from poetry and plays to essays and

Figure 16: Aleister Crowley, ca. 1925

magickal texts, as well as a world traveler, mountaineer, and practitioner of "sex magick." His lifestyle was decadent and libertine, flouting the social norms of his time, which led to widespread public disapproval and scrutiny. After an early education in evangelical Christian schools, Crowley attended the University of Cambridge. It was during his university years that he began to reject his Christian roots, diving deep into occult studies, Eastern mysticism, and ceremonial magick. In 1898, he joined the Hermetic Order of the Golden Dawn, a significant occult organization of the time. However, conflicts with other members led to his exit and subsequent formation of his own spiritual philosophy: Thelema.

In Thelema, Crowley sought to overturn traditional religious and moral values in favor of a new ethical code. The term *Thelema* is derived from the ancient Greek word θέλημα, meaning "will," which serves as a cornerstone concept for his belief system. Central to Thelemic philosophy is the maxim "Do what thou wilt shall be the whole of the Law," suggesting that individual will is the driving force behind human action and the key to true spiritual liberation. In Thelema, the concept of "True Will" is paramount. Unlike mundane desires or whims, one's True Will is viewed as the inmost divine nature that aligns with the greater cosmic will, often symbolized as the will of the god Horus for the New Aeon. By identifying and acting in accordance with one's True Will, the individual harmonizes their own actions with the cosmic order, effectively becoming a co-creator of reality rather than a subject to fate or external authority. Thelema incorporates a variety of practices and rituals aimed at helping the practitioner discover their True Will and to act in accordance with it. While it

draws from earlier arcane systems, it also introduces new gods
and symbolic systems. Key among these is *Liber AL vel Legis*
(*The Book of the Law*), a text Crowley claimed to have received
from a discarnate entity named Aiwass in 1904 (see Figure 17).
This book serves as the foundational scripture of Thelema
and introduces key Thelemic deities such as Nuit, Hadit, and
Ra-Hoor-Khuit.

While the movement was never large, Thelema's influence
has been significant, extending beyond traditional occult circles
to inspire a range of religious, artistic, and cultural expressions.
Thelemic ideas have been adapted into various forms of modern
Paganism and have influenced a wide array of spiritual and
artistic movements. As a transformative force in modern esotericism, Thelema represents a distinct reimagining of spiritual

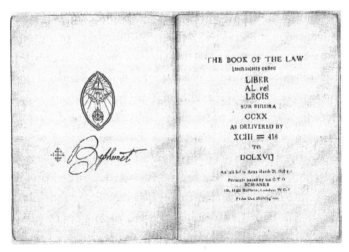

Figure 17: Front page from a published version of Liber AL vel Legis *showing*
Baphomet *written inside, ca. 1904*

principles and practices, encouraging individuals to embrace their unique path in life.

Crowley died on December 1, 1947, but left a legacy that continues to provoke and inspire to this day. His interpretation and adaptation of the symbol of Baphomet are a testament to his complex, multifaceted approach to spirituality, mysticism, and life itself. His work is an amalgam of various belief systems—borrowing elements from Eastern and Western mysticism, Kabbalistic and Hermetic wisdom, and other influences—and offers an esoteric view of Baphomet that either frustrated or enlightened his readers. The divide over his writings speaks to the broader question of the accessibility of esoteric knowledge and its role in shaping public opinion. Within this mix, the reinterpretation of Baphomet stands out as a crystalline example of Crowley's intent to challenge established religious and social norms. His vision goes beyond iconoclasm, extending into the creation of a coherent system that raises numerous questions about spirituality, meaning, and the capacity for symbols to evolve over time. Given Crowley's propensity for controversy, it's no surprise that his version of Baphomet has sparked debate. The critiques range from accusations of distorting historical traditions to superficial engagement with gender fluidity and androgyny. Crowley's Baphomet challenges both historical interpretations and modern appropriations, revealing how fluid and contested such symbols can be (Pasi 2013). However, what cannot be denied is that Crowley's Baphomet has left an indelible mark on modern esotericism. It serves not merely as an object of worship or ritual but as a symbol embodying key tenets of Thelemic thought, such as the union of opposites and the transcendence of earthly dualities.

One of the essential questions this chapter aims to explore is the "ownership" of symbolic meaning. Does Baphomet belong to the realm of historical context, fixed in meaning by its creators, or does it possess the flexibility to adapt and evolve? It is a question that not only applies to Crowley but also sets the stage for subsequent reinterpretations of Baphomet in contemporary occultism, a theme we will pick up in Chapter 6. As we proceed, the central question remains: What does it mean when a symbol as potent as Baphomet is subjected to the interpretive will of a figure as polarizing as Aleister Crowley? Crowley's reinterpretation of Baphomet represents a seismic shift in how the symbol has been understood within religious contexts. Unlike contemporary Christian views, where Baphomet is often classified as a demonic figure, Crowley's Thelema positions it as a unifying symbol that transcends duality. He viewed Baphomet as the representation of "the Devil" that encapsulates unity, enlightenment, and balance. Crowley states in *Magick in Theory and Practice*:

> *"The Devil" is, historically, the God of any people that one personally dislikes. This has led to so much confusion of thought that THE BEAST 666 has preferred to let names stand as they are, and to proclaim simply that AIWAZ, the solar-phallic-hermetic "Lucifer," is His own Holy Guardian Angel, and "The Devil" SATAN or HADIT, the Supreme Soul behind RA-HOOR-KHUIT the Sun, the Lord of our particular unit of the Starry Universe. This serpent, SATAN, is not the enemy of Man, but He who made Gods of our race, knowing Good and Evil; He bade "Know Thyself!" and taught*

Initiation. He is "the Devil" of the Book of Thoth, and
His emblem is BAPHOMET, the Androgyne who is the
hieroglyph of arcane perfection. (Crowley 1913)

Here, Crowley liberates the figure of Baphomet from its demonic associations and elevates it to the level of cosmic, even divine, significance. The impact of Crowley's theological reinterpretation is multilayered, sparking both admiration and opposition. While it opens up fertile ground for theological exploration, the departure from established belief systems has also led critics to question the validity and sincerity of Crowley's interpretation. Yet the fact remains that his rendition of Baphomet has left an indelible mark on modern occultism and spiritual philosophy.

Another differentiating aspect of Crowley's Baphomet lies in its representation of both masculine and feminine traits. This was an audacious move, challenging the predominant religious symbols and norms of his time, which were often patriarchal in nature. The dual nature of Baphomet in Crowley's framework can be likened to his overarching philosophy of unity beyond duality—a theme closely mirrored in the Gnostic mass performed by the Ecclesia Gnostica Catholica (EGC), the ecclesiastical arm of the Ordo Templi Orientis (O.T.O.), an international fraternal initiatory organization dedicated to the Law of Thelema. Crowley integrated Baphomet into Thelemic rituals and ceremonies like the Gnostic mass (Bogdan and Starr 2012) but did not directly invoke it; rather, the ritual itself served as a tribute to the unification of opposites (see Figure 18). The magickal formulae used in Thelemic practices, such as INRI and IAO, correlate to the transformative aspects of Baphomet, which is frequently depicted with the Latin words *solve* and *coagula*.

PHOTO BY ARNOLD GENTHE, N.Y.

Figure 18: Aleister Crowley as Baphomet X° O.T.O.
Photograph: Arnold Genthe. Source: The Equinox 3.1
(Detroit: Universal Publishing Company, 1919).

The Product of an Age

Crowley's unique rendition of Baphomet didn't emerge in a
vacuum; it was part of the broader nineteenth-century occult
revival that swept through Europe and North America. In
a world teetering on the brink of modernity yet still deeply
rooted in Victorian values, occultism offered an enticing middle
ground between the waning influence of traditional religious

institutions and the ascendant scientific rationalism (Owen 2004). From Rosicrucianism to Spiritualism, this period witnessed an explosion of interest in esoteric subjects, spurred by figures like Éliphas Lévi, Helena Blavatsky, and later, Crowley himself (ibid.).

At the crossroads of Thelema and Baphomet, Crowley's interpretation adds yet another layer to this already complex symbol. Whether one views Crowley as a mystical savant or a manipulative charlatan, his version of Baphomet has irrevocably shifted the symbol's position within the esoteric landscape. The question of artistic intent versus public interpretation remains a moot point; Baphomet, as a symbol, seems to defy the constraints of singular ownership or meaning, continually evolving with each new interpretation. Crowley's multifaceted (theological, social, and political) interpretations of Baphomet demonstrate the fluidity and adaptability of such a symbol. It is clear that Crowley's Baphomet is not a mere carbon copy of Lévi's original concept; rather, it is a strategic departure that has infused the symbol with layers of meaning relevant to Crowley's time, beliefs, and agenda. Moreover, his radical departures in the use and interpretation of Baphomet ignite a provocative question: Who owns the meaning of art and symbolism after its creation? Lévi, Crowley, and—as we will see in Chapter 6—Anton LaVey and other modern occultists have each co-opted and redefined Baphomet to align with their respective visions. Does the artist's original intent matter, or do symbols like Baphomet take on a life of their own upon their introduction into the collective psyche?

The reinterpretations and appropriations of Baphomet symbolize a broader tension between artistic intent and societal redefinition—a tension that is particularly relevant as we enter an era in which the boundaries between traditional religion, modern spirituality, and popular culture become increasingly porous. As Chapter 6 will explore, the symbol of Baphomet continues to evolve, appearing in various forms across contemporary occult groups and beyond. While the thematic consistency of the unity of opposites remains, its meaning, use, and cultural implications are subject to the whims of each new interpreter. In many ways, Baphomet serves as a microcosm of the challenges and opportunities faced by the evolving human endeavor to make sense of the universe through symbols, myths, and rituals.

Crowley's interpretation of Baphomet as a unifying, androgynous figure representing the synthesis of opposites was initially met with intrigue but also considerable skepticism within occult circles. His focus on the elements of sexual mysticism and androgyny was groundbreaking yet also deeply challenging to traditional religious views and symbols of the era (Urban 2006). Occult practitioners who were influenced by more conservative spiritual traditions found Crowley's Baphomet uncomfortable, even heretical. To them, Crowley seemed to be hijacking a symbol already suffused with mystery and controversy and steering it into even murkier waters. On the other hand, younger, more avant-garde occultists found in Crowley's Baphomet a liberating symbol that broke free from what they saw as the stultifying, moralistic interpretations of the past. They felt that Crowley's work, steeped in modern psychology and Eastern mysticism, represented a leap forward for Western esoteric thought. For these individuals, Crowley's reworking of the Baphomet symbol fitted well into the broader framework of the emerging "New Age" thinking that was beginning to emerge, blending occultism with psychology, science, and social activism.

Crowley was no stranger to controversy; his interests and activities spanned not just the realm of spirituality but also the spheres of politics and social norms. His utilization of Baphomet serves as a testament to this dual influence. Crowley's Baphomet could be viewed as a radical form of social commentary, challenging established religious and societal norms. His counter-cultural stance and iconoclastic approach were not intended solely to cause upheaval but rather to stimulate a societal reevaluation of long-held beliefs and moral certainties. The subversive power of Baphomet within Thelema goes beyond mere shock value; it functions as a vehicle to question the status quo and upend conventional wisdom. Critics argue that Crowley's interpretations are opportunistic, designed to maximize his own social impact and notoriety. However, proponents contend that his understanding of Baphomet brought to the fore issues that were otherwise marginalized or suppressed, effectively shaking the foundations of traditional religious and social thought.

Crowley's writing on Baphomet abounds with complexities that require a comprehensive grasp of Kabbalistic, Hermetic, and Thelemic thought (DuQuette 2003). His take on Baphomet navigates multiple layers of meaning, moving from the surface-level iconography to deeply esoteric and mystical interpretations. For instance, Crowley's frequent references to Kabbalistic symbolism in his works provide a nuanced lens through which to understand Baphomet. His complex renditions may confound the uninitiated, but they offer a rich source of insights for those well versed in esoteric studies. Whether viewed as profound wisdom or as deliberate obfuscation, however, Crowley's esoteric interpretations of Baphomet remain an intricate part of his lasting legacy.

Understanding Crowley's version of Baphomet necessitates a look into the zeitgeist of his era. It serves as both a critique and a product of its time, woven into the intellectual and spiritual fabric of the early twentieth century. Crowley operated within a complex network of religious, philosophical, and occult movements that both influenced and were influenced by his work. His interactions with other prominent figures of his time—such as Samuel Liddell MacGregor Mathers, founder of the Hermetic Order of the Golden Dawn—add yet another dimension to his interpretation of Baphomet. The general public's reaction to Crowley and his version of Baphomet was largely shaped by the media of the day, which often portrayed him as "the wickedest man in the world" (Symonds and Grant 1989). Newspapers and magazines, intrigued and horrified by the exotic rituals and libertine lifestyle that surrounded Crowley, often zeroed in on his use of symbols like Baphomet as proof of his sinister intentions. The complex theological and philosophical nuances of Crowley's Baphomet were largely lost in these sensationalistic portrayals, reducing a deeply multifaceted symbol to a byword for moral panic. Despite this, or perhaps because of it, Crowley's influence has endured, with his interpretations infiltrating not just esoteric orders but also popular culture, from music to fashion to literature.

The figure of Baphomet has undergone yet another transformation—from feared devil to occult symbol to a modern representation of resistance against religious orthodoxy and social conformity. Each new generation finds in Baphomet, and in Crowley's complex, controversial legacy, a mirror of its own anxieties, aspirations, and eternal quest for spiritual illumination. The Baphomet of Aleister Crowley diverges substantially from Lévi's earlier interpretation. This divergence is not merely a matter of theological or symbolic nuance; it marks a significant redefinition of the symbol's essence. This sets the stage for the next chapter, where we explore how Baphomet has been reappropriated in contemporary times by figures like Anton LaVey, raising questions about who owns the meaning of art once it is created.

Chapter 6

THE NEW ERA
Baphomet in Contemporary Occult
Groups and Beyond

Symbols are only the vehicles of communication;
they must not be mistaken for the final term,
the tenor, of their reference.

—JOSEPH CAMPBELL, American scholar and mythologist

Baphomet's symbolism has ignited a firestorm of legal battles
and controversies, especially in the United States. From court-
rooms to public squares, the depiction of Baphomet has found
itself at the center of debates surrounding religious freedom,
cultural appropriation, and copyright issues. Yet, amid this
cacophony, one could argue that Baphomet is undergoing a
metamorphosis—transforming from an elusive figure lurking in
the shadows of occult practices to a symbol that challenges, perhaps even defies, established cultural and religious norms. As we
proceed through this chapter, we'll explore these various facets
of Baphomet's contemporary manifestations. We'll examine the
symbol's incorporation into modern fashion and music, eval-
uate its relevance in twenty-first-century occult practices, and

scrutinize the legal wranglings that have put Baphomet at the intersection of law and culture. What remains constant, however, is the symbol's uncanny ability to incite fascination, stir debate, and capture imaginations.

A memorable event that took place on a fateful Saturday in 2015 reinvigorated the presence of Baphomet in popular culture. As the clock neared midnight, approximately seven hundred people convened in a repurposed industrial warehouse near the Detroit River for what was heralded as the "largest public satanic ceremony in history" (Jenkins 2015). The congregation was a diverse group of individuals, some of whom openly identified with modern Satanism—a religious category often misunderstood and misrepresented—and others motivated by sheer curiosity. Contrary to the sensationalized portrayals of Satanists as nefarious figures engaged in dark rituals, the atmosphere of the event resembled a "a cross between an underground rave and a meticulously planned Halloween party" (ibid.). The centerpiece of this unique gathering was the unveiling of a monumental bronze statue of Baphomet.

The craftsmanship of the statue was both intricate and laden with symbolism. Towering at nearly nine feet and weighing close to a ton, the figure was seated on a throne emblazoned with a pentagram. The statue sported robust ram horns, a muscular physique, wings, and hooves instead of human feet. Adding an unexpected layer of complexity were two bronze children, a boy and a girl, standing on either side of Baphomet, gazing at the figure in earnest wonder.

According to Jex Blackmore, the event's organizer and a key figure in the Detroit chapter of the Satanic Temple, Baphomet serves as a harmonizing force, embodying the reconciliation of opposites and challenging the boundaries of religious tolerance in the United States (ibid.). The Satanic Temple, under Blackmore's leadership, has emerged as a structured entity within the otherwise fragmented landscape of Satanism. While the organization resists easy categorization as either a religious or anti-religious group, it coheres around a set of principles that emphasize rationality, humaneness, and the reduction of unnecessary suffering. The unveiling of the Baphomet statue was not merely an artistic or religious endeavor but also a political act of defiance. Originally intended to be displayed alongside a Ten Commandments monument at the Oklahoma State Capitol, the statue became a focal point in the ongoing debate over the separation of church and state (ibid.).

While the Detroit event served as a groundbreaking moment in the public discourse surrounding Baphomet and religious freedom, it was by no means an isolated incident. The complexities of religious pluralism and constitutional freedoms extend beyond the boundaries of a single state or community. This becomes abundantly clear when we turn our attention to a parallel event that unfolded in Arkansas. There, the Satanic Temple once again found itself at the epicenter of a contentious debate over religious monuments and the public sphere, but with unique legal and social challenges that further enrich our understanding of Baphomet's multifaceted role in contemporary American society. At a First Amendment rally held at the Arkansas State Capitol that drew national attention, the Satanic Temple orchestrated the unveiling of a statue of the goat-headed, winged Baphomet. The rally was organized in opposition to a Ten Commandments monument already situated on the Capitol grounds (Grabenstein 2018).

The gathering was a microcosm of America's religious and philosophical diversity, featuring Satanists, atheists, and Christians alike. Multiple speakers at the event advocated for either the removal of the Ten Commandments monument or the installation of the Baphomet statue as an alternative. The Satanic Temple argued that the existing monument infringed upon constitutional freedoms relating to religion and contended that the placement of their statue would serve as a testament to religious tolerance (ibid.). Ivy Forrester, cofounder of Satanic Arkansas and one of the rally's organizers, captured the sentiment succinctly: "If you're going to have one religious monument, then the space should be open to others. If that's not agreeable, then perhaps no monuments should be displayed at all" (ibid.).

The Ten Commandments monument, sponsored by Republican Sen. Jason Rapert, had its own turbulent history. Within a day of its installation, it was destroyed by an individual who drove his car into it. This same person had previously demolished a similar monument in Oklahoma, where the Satanic Temple had initially sought to place its Baphomet statue. Following a ruling by Oklahoma's Supreme Court that deemed the Ten Commandments monument unconstitutional, the Satanic Temple suspended its efforts in that state (Jacobs 2018a). Rapert, in an online statement, acknowledged the protesters' First Amendment rights but labeled them "extremists," vowing that "it will be a very cold day in hell" before a statue deemed offensive would be permanently erected at the Arkansas State Capitol (ibid.). Approximately 150 individuals attended the Arkansas rally, which was closely monitored by law enforcement. A smaller contingent of counterprotesters, carrying signs with

Bible verses, maintained a quiet presence, periodically singing hymns. The event concluded peacefully, despite a brief interruption by a vocal counterprotester who was promptly escorted away by the police (ibid.).

The events in Arkansas, marked by legal battles and public rallies, underscore Baphomet's dynamic role in the complex interplay of law, religion, and public sentiment in contemporary America. They are part of a bigger picture that highlights the historical, spiritual, and cultural dimensions of this controversial figure. While the legal and political arenas offer one vantage point, the symbol's influence is far more pervasive, extending into the very fabric of modern society.

Our journey through the history of Baphomet has taken us from the shadowy recesses of medieval European mysticism to the secretive realms inhabited by occult luminaries such as Éliphas Lévi and Aleister Crowley. We've navigated the complex intellectual and spiritual terrains that have shaped this symbol, dissecting its religious, philosophical, and esoteric underpinnings. Each historical layer adds depth to our understanding, revealing a symbol that is both ancient and continually evolving. As we turn our attention to the contemporary era, the narrative surrounding Baphomet expands and diversifies. The symbol has broken free from the confines of esoteric manuscripts and ritualistic practices, finding new life in the mainstream (see Figure 19). Today, Baphomet's visage graces not only the banners of religious freedom activists but also spaces as varied as haute couture runways and the pulsating stages of rock concerts, becoming a cultural icon in its own right. Its widespread adoption by artists and creators is not merely aesthetic but also laden with cultural and philosophical implications. Many in the fashion and music industries have incorporated elements of Baphometic symbolism into their work as a form of commentary or critique on a society still largely influenced by Judeo-Christian norms. The symbol's inherent shock value serves as both an artistic statement and a challenge to conventional mores. Yet this mainstreaming of Baphomet raises a series of compelling questions that invite further scrutiny. Does the symbol's ubiquity in popular culture dilute its rich esoteric heritage, reducing it to a mere trope? Or, conversely, does this widespread exposure represent a form of cultural evolution, a reimagining that imbues the symbol with new layers of meaning and relevance? These questions are not merely academic; they touch on the very essence of how symbols transform and adapt over time, reflecting the shifting landscapes of belief, culture, and identity.

Figure 19: Exhibition room of the Dalheim Monastery Foundation. LWL State Museum for Monastic Culture, Special Exhibition: "Conspiracy Theories—Past and Present," Illustrations: Stab-in-the-Back Myth, Baphomet, Photograph: LWL/Alexandra Buterus, ca. 2019.

This chapter not only will chronicle Baphomet's modern journey but will also raise a significant question: Who owns the meaning of art once it is created? Can a symbol, especially one as loaded as Baphomet, ever remain static, confined to the original intentions of its creator? Or does it, by virtue of entering the collective consciousness, embark on a life of its own—subject to reinterpretation, redefinition, and even reinvention? As we explore these themes, we'll be guided by the scholarly foundations laid in previous chapters. Our journey here will prepare us for Chapter 7, which will examine Baphomet's role in future esoteric traditions, extending the discourse into what lies ahead. The objective here is not merely to document the symbol's contemporary incarnations but to provide a lens through which we can view the ever-shifting landscape of cultural symbols, collective consciousness, and individual interpretation.

With that in mind, let's plunge into the fascinating world of Baphomet's life in the twenty-first century.

Symbol of the Left-Hand Path

The Church of Satan, founded by Anton LaVey in 1966, adopted the Sigil of Baphomet as its official insignia, establishing a contemporary chapter in the symbol's complex history. LaVey's adaptation of Baphomet, based on Stanislas de Guata's version, encompasses a stylized goat head enclosed within an inverted pentagram, framed by two concentric circles containing Hebrew letters that spell out Leviathan, the biblical sea monster associated with chaos and disorder. This adaptation is not only an amalgamation of various historical elements but also a recontextualization of Baphomet within the LaVeyan satanic ideology

(LaVey 1969). LaVeyan Satanism is a religious philosophy that champions individualism, carnality, and earthly existence. In this framework, Baphomet serves as an icon that encapsulates these principles. Unlike the conventional religious understanding of Satan as the embodiment of evil, LaVeyan Satanism views Satan as a symbol of human nature and the carnal instincts that traditional religions often deem sinful. In using Baphomet as its insignia, the Church of Satan deliberately engages in an act of symbolic reclamation, taking a figure demonized by mainstream religions and redefining it in accordance with its own values (Gilmore 2007).

Baphomet's role in LaVeyan Satanism goes beyond mere visual representation to also provide an ideological compass for the Church's teachings. Baphomet's dualistic nature—part human, part animal; male and female; spiritual and carnal—encapsulates the Church's approach to human experience. For LaVeyan Satanists, the symbol serves as a constant reminder of the religion's emphasis on reconciling and embracing these dualities, rather than viewing them as conflicting or antagonistic (LaVey 1976).

Public reactions to the Church of Satan's usage of Baphomet have been diverse, to say the least. The symbol has been met with fascination, revulsion, and legal contention. As described previously, its appearance in public spaces has triggered lawsuits centered on religious freedom, establishing the Church's Baphomet as not just a religious but also a legal symbol, a point of intersection where theological ideologies meet legal frameworks (Baddeley 2016). Moreover, the Church of Satan's adoption of Baphomet has had a ripple effect across various subcultures and alternative religious movements. It has prompted other Left-Hand Path and occult organizations to reexamine and incorporate Baphometic symbolism in diverse ways, thereby contributing to the figure's continually evolving role in contemporary spirituality and culture (Faxneld 2017). The concept of the Left-Hand Path in esoteric traditions refers to a branch of occultism that emphasizes the individual's self-assertion and rejects conventional religious morality and societal norms. This path is often associated with the pursuit of spiritual freedom and personal power, challenging the status quo of spiritual practice.

From religious sects to legal forums, the significance of Baphomet has traversed various domains, continuously adapted to fit changing contexts. As we move away from institutionalized forms of spirituality, the symbol finds a new canvas on which to exert its iconoclastic force: the world of fashion and aesthetics. Here, Baphomet becomes more than a mere symbol; it transforms into a compelling statement on rebellion, individuality, and the eternal questioning of societal values.

The Iconography of Rebellion

The migration of Baphometic imagery into the fashion world can be viewed as yet another layer of its complex, ever-changing narrative. For the fashion-conscious, the use of Baphomet often acts as a commentary on anti-establishment values or an allegiance to countercultural or occult themes. By embedding such a symbol into their pieces, these brands perpetuate the motif's roots in challenging prevailing norms, even if that was not the symbol's original intent. The aesthetic application of Baphomet in these contexts also provokes conversations about the balance—or imbalance—between sacred symbolism and commercial utilization. Critics of this trend argue that the use of Baphomet in fashion trivializes a symbol rich in history and complexity. They posit that the commercialization of such a figure dilutes its essence, reducing it to another commodity in a consumerist culture. However, proponents see its use as a reinvigoration of Baphomet's core themes of duality and rebellion, arguing that its presence in fashion only amplifies the capacity to question and unsettle societal conventions. Therefore, whether one views the adoption of Baphomet in fashion as a trivialization or as a contemporary reimagining, it is undeniable that the image retains its provocative power. It has transcended historical and religious boundaries to become a symbol fluid enough to adapt to the changing landscapes of culture and aesthetics, continuing its long-standing tradition of challenging established norms.

Baphomet has also been at the center of several legal controversies. Copyright disputes and challenges around religious freedom underscore the multifarious roles this symbol plays in contemporary society. The legal battle after the Satanic Temple attempted to install the statue of Baphomet at the Oklahoma State Capitol raised important questions about religious plurality and freedom in public spaces. Although the case was ultimately settled out of court, it and similar controversies in other states brought national attention to the symbol and ignited debates on the boundaries of religious freedom in the United States. In 2018, the Satanic Temple filed a lawsuit against Warner Bros. and Netflix alleging copyright infringement over the prominent use of a goat-headed statue resembling their own Baphomet statue in the series *The Chilling Adventures of Sabrina* (Jacobs 2018b). The lawsuit was later settled, with the Satanic Temple stating that the issue had been resolved to its satisfaction (Jacobs 2018a). The case drew significant media attention and highlighted the complexities surrounding the use of religious and esoteric symbols in popular media. While some saw this as a commercial trivialization of a sacred symbol, others regarded it as a testament to Baphomet's ubiquity and adaptability (ibid.).

Furthermore, the increasingly common use of Baphomet in the arts has led to disputes around artistic freedom and intellectual property. Is the Baphomet image free for anyone to use, or should its replication be confined to certain contexts or licensed by particular organizations? Such questions have yet to be definitively answered, but they do illuminate the complexities surrounding the ownership and interpretation of religious or mystical symbols in modern culture. Whether examined from a legal, religious, or cultural perspective, the symbol of Baphomet remains enmeshed in debates that extend beyond its origins and historical significance. These legal disputes not only underscore the figure's complex role in contemporary culture but also serve as a litmus test for broader societal issues surrounding freedom, ownership, and identity.

Pop Culture

Baphomet's emergence on the silver screen and in the pages of contemporary literature adds a final exoteric layer of complexity to its already obscured history. Unlike the esoteric interpretations offered in religious and occult traditions, the film and literary industries often take considerable liberties with the symbol, sometimes reducing it to a mere shorthand for malevolent forces or the supernatural. In cinema, Baphomet figures prominently in the horror genre, usually relegated to the role of a demonic entity or a dark idol to be worshipped. Films like 2015's *The Witch* depict the symbol as an embodiment of ultimate evil, often reinforcing common misconceptions. While such portrayals may be compelling for the sake of narrative, they perpetuate a narrow and often erroneous understanding of Baphomet that aligns with cultural stereotypes rather than historical or spiritual realities (Goodrick-Clarke 2008). Similarly, literature, especially in the genres of fantasy and horror, often leans into the dark mystique of Baphomet by portraying the figure as a deity of arcane magick or a symbol of forbidden knowledge. For instance, in Clive Barker's 2009 film *Books of Blood*, Baphomet is a cryptic figure associated with grim rites and unspeakable powers. As with cinema, while these literary adaptations are compelling, they contribute to the public's persistent misunderstanding of the symbol's historical complexities. There are, however, instances where the figure of Baphomet is treated with more nuance. A growing body of academic literature is beginning to examine the symbol's multifaceted nature and its appearance in popular culture. While these works are fewer in number, they serve as a crucial counterpoint to the often-sensationalized depictions found in mainstream cinema and literature.

Baphomet's symbolism resonates in the realm of music as well, particularly within genres that embrace anti-establishment or countercultural philosophies, such as heavy metal, punk, and certain strands of hip-hop. These genres frequently employ the Baphomet image or concept as an evocative means of challenging societal norms or invoking an atmosphere of mystical rebellion. The image of Baphomet has thus found its way into album artwork, music videos, and stage performances, maintaining a sort of diabolic charisma that fits seamlessly with the often-confrontational ethos of these musical forms. Artists such as Marilyn Manson, Ghost, and Slayer have incorporated the Baphometic image in a manner that goes beyond mere shock value. For these musicians, Baphomet serves as an emblem of freedom from religious orthodoxy and a challenge to moralistic societal standards. The impact of this musical engagement with Baphometic themes can be significant, providing an alternative lens through which audiences can engage with questions of morality, identity, and the dichotomy between good and evil.

However, not all appropriations of Baphomet in music are aimed at defiance or social critique. Some musicians and artists incorporate the figure as a nod to personal spiritual journeys or as an aesthetic choice devoid of deeper symbolic meaning. In these instances, Baphomet becomes another element in the artist's toolkit, a powerful image but one shorn of its traditional context. While some argue that using Baphomet in such a cavalier manner dilutes the icon's symbolic potency, others assert that Baphomet's incorporation into popular music continues the tradition of redefining and reclaiming symbols. It allows new generations to engage with Baphomet's rich history, even if in a fragmented or recontextualized form. As with its presence in fashion, the image of Baphomet in music serves as a testament to its enduring flexibility and potency as a symbol. Whether as an icon of rebellion, a statement on the fluidity of morality, or a mere aesthetic choice, Baphomet's musical manifestations are as varied as they are impactful.

The ever-expanding reach of Baphomet into the worlds of film, literature, and music underscores the figure's lasting allure and its ability to adapt to diverse cultural milieus. In the world of music, particularly within genres that often challenge mainstream norms like heavy metal, industrial, and some avant-garde forms, Baphomet again serves as a potent symbol of rebellion and individualism. The figure's duality, embodying both divine and infernal qualities, resonates with musicians who seek to explore themes of societal discord, inner conflict, and spiritual ambiguity. For instance, the iconic heavy metal band Black Sabbath drew upon esoteric and occult themes, indirectly referencing symbols like Baphomet in their lyrics and stage setups (Wall 2008). Moreover, in extreme subgenres like black metal, the symbol often appears on album covers, in music videos, and as part of live performances (see Figure 20). While not always rigorously accurate in its historical representation, the symbol serves its purpose in challenging religious orthodoxy and social conventions.

Figure 20: A visual show projected during a God Is An Astronaut *concert, ca. 2008. Photograph: Kenny Chung. Licensed under the Creative Commons Attribution-Share Alike 3.0 Unported license.*

Emerging genres like dark wave and witch house also employ Baphometic imagery, albeit in a more aestheticized and abstract manner. Artists in these genres often use the symbol to provoke thought rather than to adhere strictly to its historical roots. This form of artistic license, while not always academically rigorous, adds another layer to Baphomet's ever-evolving public image.

By contrast, some artists invoke Baphomet in a more scholarly or reverential manner. For example, Coil, an experimental music band formed in London in 1982, was known for its deep dives into esotericism and approached Baphomet as a complex icon rather than a simple signifier of rebellion. The group's work exemplifies how the symbol can be incorporated into modern culture in a way that respects its rich history and inherent complexities.

In essence, the world of music—like cinema and literature before it—offers a vast platform where the symbol of Baphomet can be continually reinterpreted. The musical sphere, with its emphasis on emotional expression and societal critique, provides a fertile ground for the ongoing evolution of this captivating figure. Whether portrayed as a demonic entity or a misunderstood deity, Baphomet serves as a compelling artisitic device, albeit one that often suffers from oversimplification or misrepresentation. Nevertheless, Baphomet's ubiquitous presence in popular culture has not been free from controversy, as evinced by the legal battles that sometimes surround it. The contested space where art and law intersect amplifies Baphomet's function as a societal lightning rod, attracting and redirecting the cultural currents of taboo, freedom, and authority.

While the temptation to consign Baphomet to the realm of the demonic or the profane is strong, especially when we in contemporary culture are surrounded by almost comical representations of Baphomet in various forms of media, doing so would be a betrayal of the icon's more nuanced and transformative implications. Its dualistic elements—animalistic and divine, male and female, material and spiritual—urge us to contemplate the complexities of a reality that lies beyond simple binary classifications. These complexities manifest not just in our moral or metaphysical worldviews but also in our cognitive structures, such as how we categorize and understand what we perceive. Just as language starts as a set of rudimentary distinctions and progresses toward more specific categorizations, so, too, does overall perception. The colors of the spectrum, for instance, are a reference to light and dark but blur together in a mix of shades that transcend simple black and white. Occult symbols like Baphomet exist to challenge such easy categorizations. They invite us to question the rigidity of our perceptions and beliefs, to see beyond mere dualities, and to venture into the multidimensional facets of human existence. This multidimensionality, as we'll see, is not restricted by the rudimentary binary of black and white; it beckons us to embrace the entire spectrum of human experience. From the simplest of colors to the most profound of ideas, we go in search of the more nuanced "in-between" that exists beyond the easy binaries.

Chapter 7

BLACK AND WHITE THINKING
Seeing Beyond Good and Evil

History is nothing but a pack of
tricks that we play upon the dead.

—VOLTAIRE, French historian and philosopher

As ancient humans gazed at the celestial drama of light and darkness, an intuitive conceptualization of opposites took root. Early people found the most elementary metaphors for articulating existence: the polarity of light and dark, day and night, became the primordial lens through which we began to perceive and categorize our world. This budding conceptual framework was not merely an observational note in the evolution of consciousness; rather, it laid the cornerstone for a complex edifice of thought. What emerged was a binary categorization system that has pervaded our spiritual doctrines, ethical philosophies, and cultural narratives for millennia. Whether symbolized by the yin and yang, codified in Zoroastrian cosmology, or deliberated in Platonic dialogues, the human proclivity for duality is a persistent theme in our intellectual and spiritual pursuits (see Figure 21).

Figure 21: Yin and yang

Yet this division is far from innocuous. The early humans' endeavor to dichotomize elements of existence—a task undertaken with the gravity of existential implication—set the stage for the moral, ethical, and even cosmic judgments that reverberate through the chronicles of civilization to the present day. When early societies associated light with divine benevolence and darkness with malevolent forces, they sowed the seeds of a dualistic worldview in not just myth and allegory but also their views of morality. Exploring the more nuanced in-between to push our boundaries of understanding beyond simply good versus evil is at the heart of what Baphomet represents. As we navigate this complex symbol of mysterious teachings and secret wisdom, we can begin to question whether thinking in such binary terms limits our understanding of the world. Could there be a way to move beyond these restrictive black-and-white categories and see a bigger picture?

Black and White

As we ponder the question of transcending our simple notions of good and evil, it is worth taking a step back to examine the very foundations upon which we've built our understanding of the world. Consider the power of color—the visual language that has framed our world since we first looked upon the flicker of firelight and the boundless blue of the heavens. It is a concept as old as human cognition, but like Baphomet it defies simple categorization. Just as the spectral dance of colors escapes easy definition, the symbol of Baphomet challenges our binary thinking, urging us to move beyond the neat divisions of good and evil that have long confined our understanding. What follows is a journey into the heart of these paradoxes, an exploration that interrogates our most fundamental ways of seeing—both literally and metaphorically.

How we've come to name and classify colors over time reveals not just the quirks of language or culture, but something more profound about the human mind. It exposes a sort of road map that traces how our thinking has grown from the elementary to the complex, marking our evolution from primitive origins to the modern age. In their seminal book *Basic Color Terms: Their Universality and Evolution*, originally published in 1969, researchers Brent Berlin and Paul Kay posit that languages tend to acquire color terms in a hierachical, predictable sequence, starting with the most simplistic and persistent dichotomy: black and white, or dark and light (Berlin and Kay 1969/1999). As cultures evolve, the color spectrum expands to include red, followed by either green or yellow. These colors are often associated with significant natural elements or phenomena crucial for survival. Red, for instance, is commonly linked with blood, ripened fruits, or fire. Green and yellow usually have ties to plant life and the earth more generally, which is vital for sustenance. This expansion suggests a broader awareness and articulation of the world, transitioning from primal dichotomies to triadic or tetradic systems of understanding (ibid.). Eventually, as a culture matures, it identifies and names other colors like blue, brown, purple, pink, orange, and gray. These colors don't universally have immediate life-or-death significance, but they often carry symbolic or aesthetic value. Their introduction into language and thought signals a shift from basic, utilitarian categorizations to more abstract, sometimes even metaphysical, concepts (ibid.).

What is especially intriguing about Berlin and Kay's argument, commonly known as *basic color term theory*, is the cross-cultural prevalence of this pattern. While one might expect that different cultures, each with its unique environment and set of challenges, would develop vastly different ways of categorizing color, the evidence suggests otherwise. The shared pattern points toward a universal cognitive framework, suggesting that despite the apparent diversity of human cultures, our basic ways of perceiving and making sense of the world are remarkably similar. This theory offers a compelling angle to understand not just color perception but also broader cognitive processes, including the dichotomies of good and evil we've explored throughout this book. When we move beyond simple binary concepts, we are free to expand our minds into the richness of the full human experience (ibid.).

The narrative of color in human history is rife with intriguing twists and turns, perhaps none more peculiar than the story of the color orange. A latecomer to the lexicon of color, orange occupies a unique space in both the spectrum of light and the spectrum of human experience. In many early societies, things we would now identify as orange were usually described as some variation of red (like the red fox and the red-tailed hawk) or yellow-red before the widespread availability of the fruit in Europe. Similarly, in Old English and many Romance languages, the term for orange did not exist as a separate color category but was rather subsumed under red (such as *rouge* in French). The English term *orange* has roots in the ancient Sanskrit word *nāranga*, which referred to the orange tree and its fruit. As trade routes connected India to the Middle East, the term morphed into the Persian *nārang*, and eventually into the Arabic *nāranj*. When the fruit made its way to Europe through trade and exploration, European languages adapted the term further, as in Old French, where it was known as *pomme d'orenge* ("apple of orange"). This Old French term was the immediate precursor to the Middle English *orenge*, which was eventually simplified to the modern English *orange*. As the fruit grew in culinary and cultural significance, so, too, did its namesake color. By the early sixteenth century, orange had disentangled itself from its generic designation as a shade of red to become recognized in the English language as its own distinct color.

Contrast this with today's plethora of named colors. The Pantone color system, for instance, doesn't just offer us orange; it gives us options as colorful as pumpkin, flame, and apricot. Paint swatches provide a similar profusion of names, ascribing descriptors to every imaginable shade. This granularity reflects our transition from a utilitarian perspective—where basic color identification served essential functions—to a more nuanced, often subjective view that caters to aesthetics, emotional resonances, and symbolic meanings. The evolution from red to orange to pumpkin mirrors the cognitive and evolutionary journey we are on as a species. We begin with simple, binary distinctions—good and evil, light and dark—and as our understanding deepens, our language and conceptual framework do so as well. Just as the term *orange* emerged to fill a nuanced space between *red* and *yellow*, we develop more intricate moral, philosophical, and aesthetic understandings that go beyond simple dualities. These complex categories allow for a broader, richer interpretation of human experience, creating a more comprehensive map of our internal and external landscape.

Into the Orange

As we advance from basic black-and-white distinctions to a more complex palette of understanding both in color and in life, we are engaging in a process akin to growing up. This isn't merely an expansion of vocabulary or sophistication in art; it is a fundamental shift in our cognitive and spiritual development. In moving from stark contrasts to a vivid spectrum, we're not just becoming more articulate or aesthetically versatile; we're *maturing*. This maturity isn't a destination but an ongoing journey where each new shade of understanding leads us closer to a well-rounded, nuanced view of ourselves and the world around us.

Maturity, as spiritual philosopher Manly P. Hall suggested, involves a realization that the universe operates not in black-and-white terms but in a spectrum of complexities. Hall envisioned maturity as a state in which one transcends the limitations of simplistic labels, moving beyond mere categorizations to understand the intricate relationships that form the whole. In many ways, his view dovetails with the concept of "the hero's journey" as articulated by mythologist Joseph Campbell. Campbell understood maturity through the lens of mythology, where the hero must undergo trials that take them far beyond the binary worldview of their originating culture. The hero returns not just with good triumphing over evil, but with a synthesis of wisdom that transcends both (Campbell 1949/2008). Much like the mythical hero, when we venture into the less charted territories of moral and spiritual landscapes, we break free from simplistic binaries and immerse ourselves in the multitudes of human experience.

Just as the alchemists of old used intricate symbols to depict the layers of spiritual and material transformation, Lévi created Baphomet as a composite of various dualistic elements—not as an embodiment of evil, but as a symbolic complex that invites us to move past easy moral dichotomies. Lévi's illustration of Baphomet is not merely a whimsical creation but a calculated endeavor to encapsulate these ancient teachings in a form that radically snaps us out of binary thinking. When faced with Baphomet's androgyny, its blend of human and animal features, and its dualistic representation of above and below, one is compelled to abandon preconceived categories and delve into a deeper dialogue with the symbol. Those who are not ready for the journey will refuse the call and retreat into their known world in fear. Those who are ready face their initial fear to cross the rubicon of understanding, and hopefully succeed in the mastery of the task. Much like the hero of mythological lore, Baphomet has been journeying through the collective psyche, gathering layers of interpretation that reveal not just the symbol itself but also the evolving consciousness of those who encounter it.

Similarly, Carl Jung advocated for a holistic approach to self-understanding that goes beyond mere dualistic thinking. Jungian theory places great emphasis on integrating the *shadow*, that part of ourselves that we'd rather not acknowledge, into our conscious understanding. The Jungian notion of *individuation*—the process of becoming who you are meant to be—bears similarities to the process by which we refine our understanding of color shades or moral gradients. Individuation is not about choosing between good and evil, but rather about embracing the full spectrum of human capability and understanding to achieve a sort of inner alchemy. We evolve from a simple division of elements into a more sophisticated, integrated entity. Jung's psychoanalytic theories echo this call for a mature understanding of symbols and self. In his view, the road to individuation involves acknowledging and integrating these various facets of ourselves, including the parts we might categorize as "bad" or "undesirable." This parallels the Baphomet's function as a symbol that challenges us to integrate rather than segregate, to synthesize rather than dissect.

The essence of maturity, as we navigate through these dimensions of color theory, moral reasoning, and spiritual symbolism, is an ongoing dialogue between the poles of human understanding. It is a perpetual unfolding, much like the expanding Pantone color spectrum or the stages of the hero's journey. In both the fine gradations of color and the ever-evolving scope of human moral and ethical understanding, maturity is not an endpoint but a process, an evolving interplay between increasingly complex modes of thought and understanding. Thus, whether we are discussing the transition from red to pumpkin, the layered meanings behind a symbol like Baphomet, or the ongoing journey toward psychological individuation, we are speaking to the same essential truth. Maturity is a rich and nuanced process: ever-expanding and open to interpretation, challenging us to continually revise our understanding as we interact with the world around us.

Think again, for a moment, of Joseph Campbell's concept of the hero's journey, that archetypal narrative describing a cyclical path of challenges, revelations, and transformations. The hero begins in a familiar world, ventures into the unknown, and returns changed, bringing with them a boon for the community. In a similar vein, in our relationship with symbols like Baphomet, we start with ingrained, often simplistic beliefs—drawn perhaps from popular culture or religious doctrine—and as we venture into the complexities these symbols actually represent, we gain insights that enrich our wider understanding. In this light, Baphomet becomes a sort of alchemical crucible: a container for the transformative processes that accompany intellectual and spiritual maturation. Encountering and engaging with this symbol forces us to face the multiplicities within ourselves and our cultural landscapes. The goat-headed deity with its caduceus, wings, and pentagram compels us to consider dualities in a world we'd often rather see in simpler terms. It acts as a mirror to our evolving consciousness, reflecting back to us the limitations of binary categorizations while also showcasing the vast potentialities that exist beyond them.

Baphomet serves as a touchstone for our collective journey toward greater understanding and integration, urging us to question, probe, and ultimately expand our categorical thinking. As we proceed on this path—whether through basic observations, philosophical inquiry, or psychological integration—we must recognize that the journey itself is the destination. Each new subtle concept we grasp, every shadow we integrate, and all the symbols we come to understand in their full complexity become milestones on our path toward maturity. They testify to the continuous dialogue we maintain with the world, reminding us that maturity is not a state of arrival, but an unending journey toward deeper understanding.

Manly Hall also pointed to the idea of an ongoing journey toward maturity, positing that maturity is not just the result of accumulating years or experiences, but an active, participatory process of growing wisdom through an understanding of universal principles. In this context, he might suggest that a mature relationship with symbols like Baphomet would entail moving beyond the simplistic moral binaries that often define popular discussions of esoteric icons. In this unfolding journey, every shade of understanding we gain, every symbolic layer we peel back, enriches the mosaic of human experience and knowledge. As we transition from stark dichotomies to a palette of sophisticated hues, we find ourselves closer to the integrated, multidimensional maturity that figures like Hall, Jung, Campbell, and, indeed, Baphomet, encourage us to seek.

The Mysteries

While early minds partitioned their world, the philosophical origins of this drive toward complexity and integration can be traced to the mystery schools of antiquity, the fortresses of esoteric wisdom. From the Eleusinian Mysteries dedicated to Demeter and Persephone in Greece to the Kabbalistic traditions of Jewish mysticism, these institutions emphasized initiation and personal experience as the pathways to deeper truths

(Goodrick-Clarke 2008). These schools held that the Divine or the Ultimate Reality, often referred to as "the One" or "the All," transcends the boundaries of conventional dichotomies (ibid.). At this apex of understanding, concepts such as good and evil, life and death, and light and dark blend into a transcendent Unity. The teachings aimed to bring the initiate into a state of Gnosis—a direct experiential knowledge that goes beyond mere intellectual understanding. The Gnostic texts, as we discussed in Chapter 2, often speak in paradoxes and allegories, inviting the seeker to grapple with and find comfort in the mysteries of existence (Meyer 2009).

Mystery schools, with their roots in ancient Egyptian temples, Celtic oral traditions, and Greek secret academies, often serve as the custodians of ancient wisdom (see Figure 22). Their

Figure 22: Remains of Roman city buried by the eruption of Mount Vesuvius in 79 AD and excavated in modern times, depicting scenes of a Dionysiac Mystery Cult, Villa of the Mysteries Fresco, ca. 50 BCE. Photograph: Gary Todd. Licensed under the Creative Commons Public Domain Mark 1.0.

teachings focus on esoteric principles that aim to guide initiates through layers of consciousness, transcending the black-and-white thinking we find so pervasive in modern society. At the heart of their teachings is the concept of the unknown, or the Mystery (with a capital *M*). This is not merely an absence of knowledge but rather a vast expanse of potentiality and possibility, akin to the cloud of unknowing in Christian mysticism or the Ain Soph in Kabbalistic tradition. The unknown is not something to be feared but an intrinsic part of the journey toward enlightenment or Gnosis. In Plato's allegory of the cave, which has often been cited as a philosophical backdrop for these schools, the unknown is represented by the world outside the cave, full of light and shadow, complex forms, and abstract ideals.

Why do these ancient systems of thought place such emphasis on the concept of the unknown? The answer might lie in the human tendency to dichotomize, to create opposites where complexities could exist. The idea of embracing the unknown challenges us to move beyond such simplistic categorizations and linear thinking. In traditions like Hermeticism, the unknown is synonymous with the All and encompasses the entirety of existence, including aspects we can't readily perceive or understand (ibid.). This embrace of the unknown fosters the development of faculties beyond mere reason, such as intuition and direct spiritual insight, offering a more holistic understanding of reality. This, then, is the fundamental message of mystery schools: the unknown is not an abyss to be feared but a realm of boundless possibilities to be explored. It serves as the ultimate testing ground for our existing paradigms, compelling us to go beyond the apparent and reach for the ineffable. Through initiatory practices, rituals, and symbolic teachings often cloaked in allegory, mystery schools aim to prepare the seeker for this quest. In doing so, they offer a different set of tools—a different color palette, if you will—for understanding and engaging with the world. In many ways, this mirrors the overarching philosophy of Baphomet as a symbol of integration and balance, unifying opposites into a harmonious whole. Just as Baphomet compels us to see beyond basic dualities, mystery schools guide us toward a deeper, more nuanced understanding of existence, a maturity that Hall, Jung, and Campbell all argued was necessary for true human flourishing. The teachings of mystery schools, then, not only echo but amplify our yearning to transcend simplistic divisions of good and evil, right and wrong, black and white. They invite us to plunge into the swirling currents of the unknown and emerge not with easy answers but with better questions, honed faculties, and a broader spectrum of understanding.

In teaching the philosophy of the unknown, various schools, such as the Eleusinian Mysteries in ancient Greece or the more modern Hermetic orders, aim to elevate human consciousness beyond the realm of superficial understanding. These teachings often involve intricate rituals and coded language meant to bypass the rational mind, tapping into a deeper, more intuitive form of knowing (Dodds 1951). By emphasizing the importance of the unknown, these institutions challenge the initiate to move beyond their comfort zone, fostering growth both intellectually and spiritually. The Kaballah, for example, posits the idea of Ain Soph, the unknowable aspect of God (Scholem 1974). Testimonials from initiates often speak of a transformative experience, describing a deep shift in their perception of reality and their place within it. While some might attribute this change to simple psychology, the initiate sees it as a profound spiritual awakening. They come to understand that there is much about existence that remains elusive, and this humble recognition is paradoxically seen as a higher form of wisdom (Hanegraaff 1997).

Through this lens, Baphomet—a symbol often misunderstood and considered frightening—can be interpreted as a nuanced emblem of this mysterious wisdom. Baphomet embodies the reconciliation of opposites, the amalgamation of disparate elements into a unified whole. Just as initiates of mystery schools are encouraged to embrace the unknown, the figure of Baphomet reminds us of the power and potential that lies in transcending binary distinctions. In a sense, the teachings of the mystery schools and the symbol of Baphomet converge on the same philosophical underpinning: the importance of dwelling in the unknown as a form of advanced intellectual and spiritual maturity.

Dwelling in the Unknown

Dwelling in the unknown was not about courting obscurity but rather embracing the limitations of human understanding. The mystery schools taught that the unknown is not a void, an absence, but rather a *plenum*—an overflowing fullness that the human mind can scarcely comprehend (Hancock 1993). Ancient Egyptian mystery schools, for example, placed significant emphasis on the concept of *Ma'at*, which can be loosely translated as "order" or "balance." Ma'at was not merely about the struggle between good and evil but represented a more nuanced understanding of cosmic equilibrium (ibid.). In such a schema, the dark is as necessary as the light, as each finds meaning only in relation to the other (Assmann 2002). Initiates would undergo rigorous training, which often involved meditation, contemplation, and other practices designed to shake the foundations of their preconceived notions. One of the more challenging and transformative aspects of this training was learning to transcend dualistic thinking. The dualities of profane and sacred, inner and outer, and microcosm and macrocosm were examined and deconstructed. Initiates were taught to see these as mere starting points for a more profound understanding of unity, where opposites coalesce into a harmonious whole (ibid.).

Likewise, the Middle Way in Buddhism is a valuable framework for developing a more integrated and mature perspective on the manifold experiences that make up human existence. By learning to embrace uncertainty and ambiguity, we can free ourselves from the limitations of binary thinking and expand our cognitive and spiritual horizons. The Buddha's doctrine of the Middle Way is a central tenet in Buddhist philosophy. It exhorts individuals to navigate a course between the two extremes of sensual indulgence and self-mortification. This teaching arose from the Buddha's own experiences. After years of practicing severe asceticism, he realized that neither extreme physical denial nor indulgence would lead to enlightenment. Instead, he advocated for a balanced life that embraces neither extreme (Rahula 1959).

In a broader sense, the Middle Way can be extrapolated to mean avoiding dualistic extremes in all aspects of life and thought. It is not merely a moral or ethical doctrine but a profound philosophical stance that touches on everything from politics and social interaction to metaphysics and spirituality.

One could argue that it advocates for the same kind of integrated wisdom presented by Hall, Campbell, and Baphomet—a nuanced understanding that transcends dichotomous thinking (Thurman 1984). By aligning with the Middle Way, individuals are encouraged to live in the "gray areas" of experience and thought, which are often the most fertile ground for personal growth and collective transformation.

Quantum Realms

These ancient attitudes are not relics of a superstitious past; they are also supported in the present and potentially the scientific future. Quantum mechanics, the theory that describes the behavior of matter and energy at these infinitesimally small scales, offers an intriguing metaphorical framework for understanding the limitations of binary thinking and the necessity of embracing a more complex, nuanced approach to existence. At the subatomic level, the very fabric of reality operates under rules that contradict our everyday experiences and challenge the classical, Newtonian view of the universe. Quantum mechanics introduces us to a realm where particles can exist in multiple states simultaneously, a phenomenon known as *superposition*. In a famous thought experiment embodying this principle, Erwin Schrödinger's cat is both alive and dead until observed (Schrödinger 1935). Superposition not only forces us to reconsider our assumptions about the nature of matter and energy, it also serves as a compelling metaphor for the limitations of binary thinking. If a particle can be in more than one state at once, why should we insist on defining experiences, ideas, or even symbols like Baphomet strictly as good or evil, right or "wrong"? Much like the mystery schools and the Middle Way, quantum mechanics encourages us to accept ambiguity and complexity as inherent features of reality.

Consider, too, the concept of *quantum entanglement*, where particles that have interacted with each other remain connected over any distance, such that the state of one instantaneously influences the state of another. This interconnectedness belies a simplistic, dualistic view of the world and underscores a more holistic, integrated perspective (Bell 1964). So, while quantum mechanics challenges the very foundations of classical physics, it also offers us an enriching metaphor for the cognitive and spiritual maturity we're discussing. It reminds us that, to reach a fuller understanding of the complexities of human experience, we must be willing to move beyond simplistic categories and binaries. The study of quantum phenomena, much like the exploration of ancient symbols and philosophical traditions, requires a capacity for holding multiple truths and navigating ambiguities—a skill that is increasingly essential as we advance along our collective journey toward greater understanding and integration.

As we grapple with the lessons of quantum mechanics, pushing the boundaries of our conventional thought patterns, another scientific paradigm waits to enrich our understanding further. Like the unsettling paradoxes of quantum superposition and entanglement, *chaos theory* also offers a lens to examine the intricate web of variables that construct our reality. What happens when we approach the very limits of predictability and stability? What wisdom might lie at the *edge of chaos*, that fine boundary separating order from disorder?

A concept originating in the study of nonlinear dynamics, chaos theory is an area teeming with potential for novel ideas and solutions. Researchers like Stuart Kauffman (1995) have studied it in the context of biological systems, suggesting that life itself thrives in these "sweet spots" of complexity. A system at the edge of chaos is neither too rigid nor too random; it hovers in a state of sublime equilibrium. The edge of chaos is not merely a state but a process—an ongoing negotiation between the forces of structure and the agents of change. Just as a pencil balanced on its point will inevitably tilt and fall, systems at the edge of chaos are inherently unstable, yet it is precisely their instability that allows for innovation and adaptation. This makes the edge of chaos a compelling metaphor for human existence and personal development: it represents a space of untapped potential. It is a reminder that creativity, novelty, and transformative change are most likely to occur when we're willing to embrace complexity and step into the unknown. To ignore or avoid this chaotic realm is to settle for a life confined to the most primitive forms of understanding, akin to perceiving the world only in black and white. The edge of chaos beckons us toward a more mature state of being, pushing us to transcend the limitations of binary thought patterns to pursue a richer, fuller, and far more nuanced experience of the world.

In the early days of my research, I was fascinated yet somewhat skeptical when I ventured into the study of historical occultists such as John Dee, Edward Kelly, and, especially, Éliphas Lévi. These were men who occupied murky realms—seemingly poised on the edge of moral acceptability, their work touching on angels, demons, and magick. As someone committed to academic rigor, I could have easily dismissed these figures as mere relics of a superstitious past, assigned them a negative or positive value, and moved on. I recall having a bit of an existential crisis after a deep dive into Dee's angelic conversations and Kelly's scrying techniques. I could understand the disagreements between the two with regard to the nature of the entities Dee was contacting. Where are they good or bad? Are the entities contacted through Enochian magic angels or demons? Christ advised, "Ye shall know them by their fruits" (Matthew 7:16–20, KJV). My journey to understand the crossroads of good and evil and to gain the wisdom of discernment led me to the works of other magicians. When I encountered Lévi's work, I was forever changed. It felt like I was finally finding answers to the questions I was grappling with in my own thought process.

There is a rare but transformative moment in the act of reading, a moment so profound that it transcends the very medium of ink and paper to evoke a deeply visceral response. This is not a mere intellectual exercise; it is a holistic experience that engages the reader's entire being—mind, body, and soul. So intense is this revelation that it disrupts the very act of reading, compelling the reader to close the book, as if to catch their breath or recalibrate their understanding of the world. It's akin to a scene from my favorite film from the eighties, the cult classic *The NeverEnding Story*. In a pivotal scene, the young protagonist, Bastian, gazes into a mirror only to see the reflection of Atreyu, a character from the story he had been reading. In that brief moment, the boundary between fiction and reality becomes porous and Bastian is forced to confront an unsettling truth: he is not merely an observer but an active participant in the unfolding narrative. Overwhelmed by this revelation, he throws the book aside, exclaiming, "But it's just a story!" I had many such moments reading *Transcendental Magic: Its Doctrine and Ritual*, instances when I experienced something so compelling that I had to close the book and reconsider my own place within the complex land-scapes of academia and metaphysics. These served as a poignant reminder that the written word is not a static construct but a dynamic framework that shapes and is shaped by our conscious-ness, much like Lévi's hand-drawn black-and-white sketch of Baphomet.

What I've learned thus far from my investigations into the occult is that the supposed dualities we often cling to are rarely as black and white as they appear. When it comes to the com-plexities of spirituality, philosophy, or even historical interpre-tation, arriving at a balanced understanding demands that we venture into the gray. It demands that we resist the temptation to label something as merely good or bad. Instead, we must seek to understand its nuances, its history, its manifold meanings, and its relevance in different contexts. This shift in my perspec-tive had a domino effect, influencing not just my academic work but my personal life and teaching approach as well. It reminded me that both wisdom and folly can reside in the same spaces and that the ultimate truth often lies somewhere in the immeasur-able spectrum between polarities. This was a living, breathing example of what the occult icon Baphomet has long represented, and what this book has aimed to bring into focus. It is fitting, then, to close the book with this quote from Carl Jung: "The meeting of two personalities is like the contact of two chemical substances: if there is any reaction, both are transformed" (1964).

Your encounter with the ideas in this book is much the same. As you step away from these pages, may you take with you a newfound understanding of the intricate landscapes of your mind and of the world. May you appreciate the beauty in ambi-guity, the richness in complexity, and the transformative power of grappling with the unknown and finding ways to embrace the gray, the in-between. For as we've discovered, true maturity—whether cognitive, spiritual, or philosophical—comes not from placing ourselves within the confines of black and white but from embracing the innumerable shades that make up our human experience. Hence, we find ourselves not at an end, but at a new beginning—a gateway into realms yet unexplored, full of potential for growth, discovery, and a deeper understanding of what makes us fundamentally human. Thank you for embarking on this journey with me. May the path ahead be illuminated by the nuanced perspectives we've encountered, enriching your ongoing exploration of the complexities of human consciousness and existence.

Appendix A

BAPHOMET SYMBOLISM ANALYSIS

THE GOAT HEAD: Often symbolized as the "Sabbatic Goat," it represents duality—such as male and female, light and dark—and embodies the universal balance of opposites, a concept often explored in the occult and esoteric wisdom traditions.

PENTAGRAM ON THE FOREHEAD: The upright five-pointed star symbolizes spiritual supremacy over the four elements of matter and the physical world. It's a sign of enlightenment and the connection between divine wisdom and earthly understanding.

TORCHES BETWEEN THE HORNS: The flame or torch between the horns stands for illumination and the eternal flame of wisdom. It's a universal symbol for guidance and higher consciousness.

ANDROGYNOUS BODY: As half-male and half-female, this body symbolizes the alchemical marriage, a concept of the union of opposites. It serves as an emblem of spiritual wholeness and reconciliation of polarizing forces.

RAISED RIGHT HAND: The right hand pointing up represents spiritual creation and the divine nature of humanity. In esotericism, it is commonly used to denote spiritual authority and apotheosis.

LOWERED LEFT HAND: The left hand pointing down represents the material aspects of life and the anchoring of spirit into matter. It symbolizes the physical realities we navigate.

WINGS: The wings symbolize the ability to transcend earthly and material limitations, representing spiritual ascension and the quest for higher understanding.

ROD OR CADUCEUS: This symbol of intertwined forces again signifies balance and is often associated with medicine. The caduceus held by Baphomet emphasizes equilibrium, healing, and the intertwining of duality.

HOOVES AND HUMAN FEET: This represents humanity's earthly connection to both animal instincts and higher consciousness, bridging the earthly and spiritual realms.

CRESCENT MOONS: The light and dark crescent moons symbolize life's cycles and natural rhythms. The moons hightlight the dual nature of existence and the balance required to navigate it.

LATIN INSCRIPTION *SOLVE*: From the Latin for "loosen" or "dissolve," this inscription represents the process of deconstructing matter, taking complex structures and reducing them to their essential elements, symbolizing the removal of earthly constraints and facilitating a connection with higher consciousness.

LATIN INSCRIPTION *COAGULA*: From the Latin for "to curdle" or "to clot," this inscription refers to the process of recombining or reconstructing elements that were broken down in the process of *solve*, symbolizing the harmonious integration of spirit and matter.

BAPHOMET TIMELINE
The Evolution of the Symbol in Western Occult History to Modernity

The symbol of Baphomet has traversed varied landscapes of thought, belief, and culture. The symbol's transformation across time highlights the multifaceted nature of esoteric wisdom, revealing insights into the complex evolution of Western occult history.

Medieval origins
(twelfth and thirteenth centuries)

- Emergence of the enigma: Baphomet first appears in the early fourteenth-century trial records of the Knights Templar, which began in 1307 and continued until the order's disbanding by Pope Clement V in 1312.

- Idol of controversy: The symbol is portrayed as a bearded head or idol, linked to the Templars' supposed heretical practices.

- Veiled in obscurity: The true origin and meaning of Baphomet remain hidden, likely dating back to at least the twelfth century. The origin of the symbol remains a captivating historical mystery rooted in medieval lore.

Éliphas Lévi and the crafting of modern Baphomet (nineteenth century)

- Lévi's transformation: French occultist Éliphas Lévi introduces a hermaphroditic, goat-headed figure in his seminal two-volume work, *Dogme et Rituel de la Haute Magie*. *Dogme*, the first volume, is published in 1854 and *Rituel*, the second volume, in 1856.

- A symbol reborn: Lévi's icon represents the union of opposites and the reconciliation of the spiritual and material realms

- Spread and influence: Thanks to Lévi, Baphomet becomes a widely recognized symbol.

Aleister Crowley and the Thelemic connection (twentieth century)

- Crowley's adoption: Prominent British occultist Aleister Crowley incorporates Baphomet into his teachings as the "Great Beast," adopting the name in 1912 when he began working with the Ordo Templi Orientis (O.T.O.).

- Symbol of creativity and liberation: Baphomet symbolizes personal freedom and primal creative force in Crowley's esoteric system.

- Wider recognition: Crowley's influence solidifies Baphomet's place in modern occultism.

Modern occult and satanic movements (twentieth and twenty-first centuries)

- Contemporary resonance: Baphomet gains prominence in modern occult and satanic movements, each ascribing unique meaning to it. Anton LaVey, founder of the Church of Satan, adopted the Sigil of Baphomet as the official insignia of the Church, using it publicly in 1969.

- Symbol of rebellion: Baphomet becomes an icon of nonconformity and revolution, resonating with countercultural movements in art, literature, and music.

- Continued evolution: The symbol's interpretations continue to adapt, reflecting the diversity of contemporary Western occult thought.

Ongoing significance and the road ahead

- Lasting fascination: Fascination with the image of Baphomet continues, as it retains its mystique and ability to challenge those who gaze upon it.

- Potential future pathways: The symbol remains a dynamic and living figure, open to new interpretations, symbolizing humanity's neverending quest for enlightenment.

BIBLIOGRAPHY

Agrippa, Heinrich Cornelius. *Three Books of Occult Philosophy*. London: Forgotten Books, 1532.

Assmann, Jan. *The Mind of Egypt: History and Meaning in the Time of the Pharaohs*. New York: Metropolitan Books, 2002.

Baddeley, Gavin. *Lucifer Rising: Sin, Devil Worship, and Rock 'n' Roll*, London: Plexus Publishing, 2016.

Barber, Malcolm. *The New Knighthood: A History of the Order of the Temple*. Cambridge, UK: Cambridge University Press, 1993.

Barber, Malcolm. *The Trial of the Templars*. Cambridge, UK: Cambridge University Press, 2012.

Barruel, Augustin. *Memoirs Illustrating the History of Jacobinism*. London: T. Burton, 1797.

Bell, John S. "On the Einstein Podolsky Rosen Paradox." *Physics* 1, no. 3 (1964): 195–200.

Berlin, Brent, and Paul Kay. *Basic Color Terms: Their Universality and Evolution*. Stanford, CA: Center for the Study of Language and Information, 1999. First published 1969 by University of California Press (Berkeley and Los Angeles).

Blavatsky, H. P. *The Secret Doctrine*. Pasadena, CA: Theosophical University Press, 1888.

Bogdan, Henrik, and Martin P. Starr. *Aleister Crowley and Western Esotericism*. Oxford, UK: Oxford University Press, 2012.

Bullock, Steven C. *Revolutionary Brotherhood: Freemasonry and the Transformation of the American Social Order, 1730–1840*. Chapel Hill: University of North Carolina Press, 1998.

Campbell, Joseph. *The Hero with a Thousand Faces*. Novato, CA: New World Library, 2008. First published 1949 by Pantheon Books (New York).

Castle, Edward James. "Proceedings against the Templars in France and in England for Heresy." In *The Proceedings against the Templars in the British Isles*, 1–152. London: John Hogg, 1907.

Coil, Henry W. *Coil's Masonic Encyclopedia*. New York: Macoy Publishing & Masonic Supply Co., 1996.

Cook, Michael. *Forbidding Wrong in Islam: An Introduction.* Cambridge, UK: Cambridge University Press, 2003.

Costen, M. D. *The Cathars and the Albigensian Crusade*. Manchester, UK: Manchester University Press, 1997.

Coudert, Allison P. *The Impact of the Kabbalah in the Seventeenth Century: The Life and Thought of Francis Mercury Van Helmont (1614–1698)*. Leiden, Netherlands: Brill, 1999.

Crowley, Aleister. *Magick in Theory and Practice*. In *The Equinox* I, no. VIII. London: Simpkin, Marshall, Hamilton, Kent & Co., 1913.

Da Vinci, Leonardo. *Vitruvian Man*. 1490. Pen and ink on paper. Gallerie dell'Accademia di Venezia.

Decker, Ronald, Michael Dummett, and Thierry Depaulis. *A Wicked Pack of Cards*. New York: St. Martin's Press, 1996.

De Guaita, Stanislas. *La Clef de la Magie Noire*. Paris: Chamuel, 1897.

Dodds, E. R. *The Greeks and the Irrational*. Berkeley: University of California Press, 1951.

DuQuette, Lon Milo. *The Magick of Aleister Crowley: A Handbook of the Rituals of Thelema*. San Francisco: Red Wheel/Weiser, 2003.

Dyer, Colin. *Symbolism in Craft Freemasonry: Discover the Meaning of the Masonic Rituals and Customs*. Rev. ed. Cambridgeshire, UK: Lewis Masonic, 2003.

Ellenberger, Henri F. *The Discovery of the Unconscious: The History and Evolution of Dynamic Psychiatry*. New York: Basic Books, 1970.

Faxneld, Per. *Satanic Feminism: Lucifer as the Liberator of Woman in Nineteenth-Century Culture*. New York: Oxford University Press, 2017.

Ficino, Marsilio. *The Letters of Marsilio Ficino: Volume 7*. Translated by Clement Salaman. London: Shepheard-Walwyn, 2004.

Frale, Barbara. *The Templars: The Secret History Revealed*. New York: Arcade Publishing, 2011.

Gilmore, Peter H. *The Satanic Scriptures*. Baltimore: Scapegoat Publishing, 2007.

Goodrick-Clarke, Nicholas. *The Western Esoteric Traditions: A Historical Introduction*. Oxford, UK: Oxford University Press, 2008.

Grabenstein, Hannah. "Satanic Temple Unveils Baphomet Statue at Arkansas Capitol." Associated Press, August 16, 2018. *www.apnews.com*.

Haag, Michael. *Templars: History and Myth: From Solomon's Temple to the Freemasons*. Rochester, NY: Harper Paperbacks, 2009.

Hall, Manly P. *The Secret Teachings of All Ages*. Los Angeles: Philosophical Research Society, 1928.

Hammer-Purgstall, Joseph von. *Mysterium Baphometis Revelatum.* Edited with endnotes and introduction by Tracy Twyman. Self-published, 2017. First published in 1818 (Vienna).

Hancock, Graham. *The Sign and the Seal: The Quest for the Lost Ark of the Covenant.* New York: Touchstone Publishers, 1993.

Hanegraaff, Wouter J. *New Age Religion and Western Culture: Esotericism in the Mirror of Secular Thought.* New York: State University of New York Press, 1997.

Hobsbawn, Eric J. *The Age of Revolution: Europe 1789–1848.* London: Weidenfeld & Nicolson, 1962.

Hoeller, Stephan A. *Gnosticism: New Light on the Ancient Tradition of Inner Knowing.* Wheaton, IL: Quest Books, 2002.

Holroyd, Stuart. *The Elements of Gnosticism.* Shaftesbury, Dorset, UK: Element Books, 1994.

Howard, Michael. *The Occult Conspiracy: Secret Societies—Their Influence and Power in World History.* Rochester, NY: Destiny Books, 1989.

Huson, Paul. *Mastering Witchcraft.* New York: Perigee Trade, 1980.

Hutton, Ronald. *The Triumph of the Moon: A History of Modern Pagan Witchcraft.* Oxford, UK: Oxford University Press, 2001.

Idel, Moshe. *Kabbalah: New Perspectives.* New Haven, CT: Yale University Press, 1988.

Jacobs, Julia. "Satanic Temple Settles Lawsuit Over Goat-Headed Statue in 'Sabrina.'" *New York Times,* November 22, 2018. *www.nytimes.com.*

Jacobs, Julia. "Satanic Temple Sues over Goat-Headed Statue in 'Sabrina' Series." *New York Times*, November 9, 2018. *www.nytimes.com*.

Jenkins, Nash. "Hundreds Gather for Unveiling of Satanic Statue in Detroit." *Time*, July 27, 2015. *www.time.com*.

Jung, Carl G. *Man and His Symbols*. New York: Dell, 1964.

Kauffman, Stuart. *At Home in the Universe: The Search for Laws of Self-Organization and Complexity*. New York: Oxford University Press, 1995.

King, Karen L. *The Gospel of Mary of Magdala: Jesus and the First Woman Apostle*. Salem, OR: Polebridge Press, 2003.

Knight, Thomas A. *The Strange Disappearance of William Morgan*. Brecksville, OH: Self-published, 1932.

Lambert, Malcolm. *The Cathars*. Oxford, UK: Blackwell, 1998.

LaVey, Anton Szandor. *The Satanic Bible*. New York: William Morrow Paperbacks, 1969.

LaVey, Anton Szandor. *The Satanic Rituals*. New York: Avon Books, 1976.

Lévi, Éliphas. *La Clef des Grands Mystères* [The Key of the Mysteries]. Translated by Aleister Crowley. San Francisco: Red Wheel/Weiser, 2002. First published 1861 by Ancienne Librairie Germer-Baillière et Cie (Paris).

Lévi, Éliphas. *Dogme et Rituel de la Haute Magie* [Transcendental Magic, Its Doctrine and Ritual]. Translated by A. E. Waite 1896. Eastford, CT: Martino Fine Books; Esoteric Thrifty edition, 2011. First published 1855 by Ancienne Librairie Germer-Baillière et Cie (Paris).

Lewis, Bernard. *The Assassins: A Radical Sect in Islam.* New York: Basic Books, 2002.

Littré, Émile. *Dictionnaire de la langue française.* Paris: L. Hachette, 1877.

Mack, Burton L. *The Christian Myth: Origins, Logic, and Legacy.* New York: Continuum, 2001.

Mackey, Albert. *An Encyclopedia of Freemasonry: Volume One.* Edited by William J. Hughan and Edward L. Hawkins. Foreword by Michael R. Poll. New Orleans: Cornerstone Book Publishers, 2015. First published 1873 by Moss & Co and A. G. Mackey (Philadelphia).

McIntosh, Christopher. *Eliphas Lévi and the French Occult Revival.* New York: State University of New York Press, 2011.

McIntosh, Christopher. *The Rosicrucians: The History, Mythology, and Rituals of an Occult Order.* San Francisco: Red Wheel/ Weiser, 1998.

Mead, G. R. S. *Pistis Sophia: The Gnostic Tradition of Mary Magdalene, Jesus, and His Disciples.* Mineola, NY: Dover Publications, 2005.

Meyer, Marvin W., ed. *The Nag Hammadi Scriptures.* San Francisco: HarperOne, 2009.

Michelet, Jules. *History of France.* Hamburg, Germany: Tredition Classics, 2011. First published 1847 by D. Appleton (New York).

Mirandola, Giovanni Pico della. "Oration on the Dignity of Man." Public discourse, 1486.

Moore, R. I. *The War on Heresy.* Cambridge, MA: Belknap Press of Harvard University Press, 2014.

Nelson, Benjamin. *The Idea of Usury: From Tribal Brotherhood to Universal Otherhood*. 2nd ed. Chicago: University of Chicago Press, 1969.

Neugebauer-Wölk, Monika. "Nicolai-Tiedemann-Herder: Texts and Controversies on Hermetic Thinking in the Late Enlightenment." In *Antike Weisheit und kulturelle Praxis: Hermetismus in der Frühen Neuzeit* [Ancient Wisdom and Cultural Practice: Hermeticism in the Early Modern Period], edited by Anne-Charlott Trepp and Hartmut Lehmann, 397–448. Göttingen: Vandenhoeck & Ruprecht, 2001.

Newman, Sharan. *The Real History Behind the Templars*. New York: Berkley Books, 2007.

Nicholson, Helen. *The Proceedings Against the Templars in the British Isles, Volume 2: The Translation*. 1st ed. London: Routledge, 2011.

Nicolai, Friedrich. *Beschreibung einer Reise durch Deutschland und die Schweiz, im Jahre 1781* [Description of a Journey through Germany and Switzerland in 1781]. Berlin: Self-published, 1782.

O'Shea, S. *The Perfect Heresy: The Revolutionary Life and Death of the Medieval Cathars*. New York: Walker & Company, 2000.

Owen, Alex. *The Place of Enchantment: British Occultism and the Culture of the Modern*. Chicago: University of Chicago Press, 2004.

Pagels, Elaine. *The Gnostic Gospels*. New York: Vintage Books, 1989.

Partner, Peter. *The Knights Templar and Their Myth*. Rochester, NY: Destiny Books, 1990.

Pasi, Marco. *Aleister Crowley and the Temptation of Politics*. Durham, NC: Acumen Publishing, 2013.

Pike, Albert. *Morals and Dogma of the Ancient and Accepted Scottish Rite of Freemasonry*. Washington, DC: Supreme Council, 33°, Southern Jurisdiction, 1871.

Plato. *The Republic*. Translated by Desmond Lee. New edition. London: Penguin Classics, 2007.

Potts, Daniel T. *The Arabian Gulf in Antiquity*. Oxford, UK: Clarendon, 1991.

Principe, Lawrence M. *The Secrets of Alchemy*. Illustrated edition. Chicago: University of Chicago Press, 2015.

Ragon, J. M. *Orthodoxie Maçonnique*. Paris: E. Dentu, 1853.

Rahula, Walpola. *What The Buddha Taught*. Oxford, UK: Oneworld Publications, 1959.

Ralls, Karen. *The Templars and the Grail: Knights of the Quest*. Wheaton, IL: Quest Books, 2003.

Rankin, William. "Cartography and the Reality of Boundaries." *Cartographica* 45, no. 1 (2010): 1–12.

Read, Piers Paul. *The Templars: The Dramatic History of the Knights Templar, the Most Powerful Military Order of the Crusades*. New York: St. Martin's Press, 2009.

Robinson, John J. *Dungeon, Fire and Sword*. New York: M. Evans & Company, 2009.

Scholem, Gershom. *Kabbalah*. New York: Meridian Books, 1974.

Scholem, Gershom. *Major Trends in Jewish Mysticism*. Jerusalem: Schocken Publishing House, 1941.

Schonfield, Hugh J. *The Essene Odyssey: The Mystery of the True Teacher and the Essene Impact on the Shaping of Human Destiny*. Shaftesbury, UK: Element Books, 1984.

Schrödinger, Erwin. "Die gegenwärtige Situation in der Quant-enmechanik" [The Present Situation in Quantum Mechanics]. *Naturwissenschaften* 23 (1935): 807–12.

Stocking, George W. *Victorian Anthropology*. New York: Free Press, 1987.

Strube, Julian. "The 'Baphomet' of Eliphas Lévi: Its Meaning and Historical Context." *Correspondences* 4 (2017): 37–79.

Sutin, Lawrence. *Do What Thou Wilt: A Life of Aleister Crowley*. New York: St. Martin's Griffin, 2002.

Symonds, John, and Kenneth Grant. *The Confessions of Aleister Crowley: An Autohagiography*. London: Penguin Books, 1989.

Taxil, Léo. *Les Mystères de la Franc-Maçonnerie*. Paris: Self-published, 1886.

Thurman, Robert A. F. *The Central Philosophy of Tibet: A Study and Translation of Jey Tsong Khapa's Essence of True Eloquence*. Edited by Robert A. F. Thurman. Princeton, NJ: Princeton University Press, 1984.

Trimingham, J. Spencer. *The Sufi Orders in Islam*. Oxford, UK: Oxford University Press, 1998.

Tschudy, Théodore Henry de. *L'Étoile Flamboyante ou la Société des Francs-Maçons considérée sous tous ses aspects*. [The Flaming Star or the Society of Freemasons considered in all its aspects]. Paris: Chez Antoine Boudet, 1766.

Upton, Charles. *The System of Antichrist: Truth & Falsehood in Postmodernism and the New Age*. Hillsdale, NY: Sophia Perennis, 2001.

Urban, Hugh. *Magia Sexualis: Sex, Magic, and Liberation in Modern Western Esotericism*. Berkeley: University of California Press, 2006.

von Franz, Marie-Louise. *Alchemical Active Imagination: Revised Edition*. C. G. Jung Foundation Books Series. Boston: Shambhala, 1997.

Waite, Arthur Edward. *Devil-worship in France; or, The Question of Lucifer*. Amsterdam: VAMzzz Publishing, 2016. First published 1896 by George Redway (London).

Waite, Arthur Edward. *The Unknown Philosopher: The Life of Louis Claude de Saint-Martin and the Substance of His Transcendental Doctrine*. London: R. Steiner Publications, 1901.

Wall, Mick. *When Giants Walked the Earth: A Biography of Led Zeppelin*. London: Orion, 2008.

Wright, Thomas, George Witt, and Sir James Tennant. "The Templars and the Worship of the Generative Powers." In *The Guilt of the Templars*, 2. New York: Basic Books, 1966.

Yates, Frances A. *Giordano Bruno and the Hermetic Tradition*. London: Routledge, 1964.

ABOUT THE AUTHOR

Dr. Heather Lynn is a historian of the human mind, xenoarchaeologist, adjunct professor of humanities, and author of *The Anunnaki Connection* and *Evil Archaeology*. Heather holds degrees in archaeology, information technology, and history, as well as a doctorate in education from the University of New England. Her academic work concentrates on cognitive archaeology, consciousness, artificial intelligence, symbolism, iconography, and the exploration of myth and art through a Jungian conceptual framework. Heather hosts the *Midnight Academy* podcast on YouTube and all major podcasting platforms.

When she is not teaching, writing, or otherwise exploring the mysteries of mind, space, and time, she plays the French horn in a local symphony orchestra whose performances raise money to provide art and cultural education to low-income communities. She has recently taken up the violin. Heather is also a practitioner of Krav Maga, a military self-defense system, and finds tranquility in classical and liturgical music, meditation, hiking, tennis, flower gardening, and a good cup of tea.

www.drheatherlynn.com